Praise for *The Stoic*

"Every startup founder knows that startups, no matter how successful they appear from the outside, are actually beset with setbacks. The best founders retain equanimity and energy regardless. This book shows how the philosophy of Stoicism can be directly applied to the process of building companies and making new things in the world." —Marc Andreessen, cofounder, Netscape and Andreessen Horowitz

"*The Stoic Challenge* is a beautifully engaging account of how to approach life with a particular gem of Stoic wisdom as your guide. I can see this book benefitting many people in their daily lives, and I'm sure they'll go on to recommend it to their friends."
—Donald Robertson, author of
How to Think Like a Roman Emperor

"[William B.] Irvine is a warm and friendly Stoic, and one of the great guides through the subject. His congenial writing offers strategies for the anxiety-free, supple kind of sturdiness with which we should all be greeting ourselves and the world."
—Derren Brown, mentalist, illusionist, and author of *Happy*

"*The Stoic Challenge* is the ultimate mental fitness program. You'll whip your fortitude into shape with exercises like negative visualization, reframing, and other Stoic principles and practices that have helped humans lead calmer, happier lives for millennia."
—David Heinemeier Hansson, coauthor of *Rework*

"While it's a commonplace that we can change our minds, this book shows us how we can also reframe our emotions in ways that liberate us from the grip of thoughts and feelings that can keep a good person down. A promising blend of classical Stoicism and trailblazing psychology."
—Christopher Phillips, author of *Socrates Café*

The

STOIC

CHALLENGE

*A Philosopher's Guide
to Becoming Tougher,
Calmer, and More Resilient*

William B. Irvine

W. W. NORTON & COMPANY
Independent Publishers Since 1923

"Toughness training" is not appropriate for children, teenagers, or individuals undergoing treatment for any physical or emotional condition. Readers are cautioned to consider their age and general health before undertaking any challenge described in these pages. Please consult your doctor or other health care provider (and, if you are pregnant, your ob/gyn) before making changes in your diet or exercise routine.

Copyright © 2019 by William B. Irvine

For information about permission to reproduce selections
from this book, write to Permissions,
W. W. Norton & Company, Inc.,
500 Fifth Avenue, New York, NY 10110

For information about special discounts for bulk purchases,
please contact W. W. Norton Special Sales at
specialsales@wwnorton.com or 800-233-4830

Manufacturing by LSC Communications, Harrisonburg
Book design by Daniel Lagin Design
Production manager: Julia Druskin

Library of Congress Cataloging-in-Publication Data

Names: Irvine, William Braxton, 1952– author.
Title: The stoic challenge : a philosopher's guide to becoming tougher,
calmer, and more resilient / William B. Irvine.
Description: First Edition. | New York : W. W. Norton & Company, 2019. |
Includes bibliographical references and index.
Identifiers: LCCN 2019014780 | ISBN 9780393652499 (hardcover)
Subjects: LCSH: Stoics.
Classification: LCC B528 .I78 2019 | DDC 188—dc23
LC record available at https://lccn.loc.gov/2019014780

ISBN 978-0-393-54149-6 pbk.

W. W. Norton & Company, Inc.
500 Fifth Avenue, New York, N. Y. 10110
www.wwnorton.com

W. W. Norton & Company Ltd.
15 Carlisle Street, London W1D 3BS

4 5 6 7 8 9 0

To Loretta Loeb,
for teaching me so much about courage and kindness

CONTENTS

THE STOIC CHALLENGE

A Day at the Airport

I was flying across the United States and had to make a connection in Chicago. The plane that would have taken me home was delayed by weather. When it finally arrived, we were asked to board, but as soon as we got seated, we were asked to deplane. The plane's cargo door, we were told, wasn't working properly. After we had sat in the terminal for fifteen minutes, we were asked to reboard, which we gladly did.

Ten minutes later the flight attendant made another announcement. The ground crew had successfully gotten the cargo door closed, but then someone realized that one suitcase hadn't been put on board. They opened the door to put it in but were then unable to close it again. The minor problem, in other words, had turned into a major problem. The attendant once again asked us to deplane.

Inside the terminal, the gate agent said they were going to get another plane for us, but shortly thereafter he announced that because the hour was so late, no plane would be available until morning. A groan went up from the passengers. He assured us that the airline would put us up at its own expense at a nearby hotel, an assurance that was met with even more groans. I was, I must admit, among the groaners, but then I realized what was happening: the Stoic gods had contrived this event on my behalf, as a kind of challenge. "Game on!" I said to no one in particular.

I did this because I knew from experience that by treating this setback as a challenge—by assuming, more precisely, that the Stoic gods had administered the setback as a test of my resilience and resourcefulness—I could simultaneously reduce the emotional cost of being set back and increase my chances of finding a workaround. At this point, though, some words of explanation are in order.

TO BEGIN WITH, I am not a member of some obscure religious cult. I am a modern adherent of an ancient philosophy. More precisely, I am a practicing Stoic, in the sense that I have chosen to live my twenty-first-century life in accordance with the strategies for living that were devised two thousand years ago by the Stoic philosophers Marcus Aurelius, Seneca, and Epictetus, among others.

I am not alone in making this choice. A growing number of people have realized that they lack what the ancient philosophers would have called a *philosophy of life*. Such a philosophy tells you what in life is worth having and provides you with a strategy for obtaining it. If you try to live without a philosophy of life, you will find yourself extemporizing your way through your days. As a result, your daily efforts are likely to be haphazard, and your life is likely to be misspent. What a waste!

It is important to realize that Stoicism is not a religion: its primary concern is not with our afterlife but with our time spent on Earth. That said, I should add that Stoicism is compatible with many religions, including Christianity and Islam. But here another clarification is in order. Above, I made reference to the "Stoic gods." I do not believe that these gods actually exist, as physical or even as "spiritual" beings. They are, for me, fictitious entities. By invoking them, I can transform what for many people would simply be an unfortunate setback into a kind of mind game. Doing this lets me respond to setbacks without becoming frustrated, angry, or despondent.

Those who dislike invoking imaginary gods as part of a psychological strategy may instead invoke an imaginary coach or teacher; the psychological effect will be equivalent. And those who do believe in God may proceed on the assumption that the setback in question is part of God's plan for them—or if they are Muslim, part of Allah's plan—as many Christians and Muslims already do. In what follows, I will have more to say about the Stoic test mind game and the psychological research that lies behind it, and I will give advice on how best to play the game, but first let me finish my airport story.

◉

WE WERE GIVEN HOTEL VOUCHERS and told to wait for a shuttle bus. We subsequently boarded it and soon arrived at our destination. After waiting in line at the reception desk, I was assigned a room and headed off for what I imagined would be at most four hours of sleep. My room, it turned out, was a long walk and elevator ride from the lobby, and when I opened the door, I saw that it was in a state of disarray.

Had I not been a Stoic, I would at this point have broken into righteous anger: *How stupid is this? How dare they?* By thinking of it as part of a challenge by the Stoic gods, though, I had a rather different thought: *What a clever wrinkle! I hadn't seen this coming. Well played, Stoic gods!* I retraced my steps back to the front desk and explained the situation to the clerk.

Had I gotten angry at him, everyone, including the clerk, would have understood. But would getting angry have been worth the price? Clearly not, if what I valued was my equanimity. It also helped me stay calm to think of the clerk not as a malicious person but merely as a bit player in this challenge that the Stoic gods had devised for me.

The clerk gave me the key for a room that, he assured me, "ought to be clean." This prediction turned out to be correct. I got what sleep I could and went down in the early morning to board the shuttle that was taking us back to the airport. It carried mostly passengers from my canceled flight, and they spent the ride trying to top each other in their complaints about the airline, the airport, and the hotel. As I watched all this, I felt lucky not to be sharing their disgruntled state of mind.

I reflected on what a bunch of spoiled brats we twenty-first-century humans are. Here we were in a climate-controlled bus, heading toward a climate-controlled airport, so we could fly across the country in a climate-controlled airplane. Should we experience thirst on that flight, someone would bring us the beverage of our choice, and if the flight was long enough, someone would offer us food. Should our bowels move, there would be a flush toilet just down the aisle. And not to be forgotten, the toilet in question would in all likelihood have toilet paper.

What, I wondered, would the American pioneers have thought of us? They might, during their lifetime, have crossed the country, but their journey would have involved wagons, weeks of discomfort, and perhaps encounters with (understandably) hostile Native Americans. Yes, the seats on those wagons would have been roomier than modern airplane seats, but many pioneers would have walked instead of ridden. These walkers might have wanted to avoid putting any additional strain on their already-overloaded wagons. Or they might simply have preferred walking to being jostled around by the wagon's bumpy ride. Back then, after all, there were no superhighways; indeed, in many places there were barely even rutted roads. Oh, and not to be forgotten, on this many-weeks-long journey, there would have been neither toilets nor toilet paper! What we modern fliers were experiencing, even with our recent setbacks, would to them have been a miracle. And yet here we were, whining about our discomfort and life's unfairness.

Our replacement plane took off and landed without further incident. At my home airport, I found my car where I had left it—whew!—and drove to my house without encountering any figurative or literal roadblocks. On arriving home, I concluded that the test was over, so I graded my performance. I had done quite well, I thought, in remaining calm and collected despite the various provocations I had been presented with. I therefore felt victorious. "Chalk one up for me," I said to no one in particular. It was unlikely, I thought, that my fellow passengers emerged from our stranding with this upbeat attitude. I have used this setback-response strategy on many occasions, with similar results.

FOR MANY OF US, becoming frustrated or angry is the natural response to not getting what we want—getting angry is just what we do. Fortunately, an alternative response exists. It is both easy to use and remarkably effective. I call it the *Stoic test strategy*: when faced with a setback, we should treat it as a test of our resilience and resourcefulness, devised and administered, as I have said, by imaginary Stoic gods. Their goal in throwing these curveballs our way is to make our days not harder but better. This statement is, I realize, paradoxical, but trust that in the pages that follow, I will explain why we should be thankful for being tested in this manner.

As its name implies, the Stoic test strategy was invented by the ancient Stoics. Yes, the Stoics were philosophers, but in the ancient world, philosophers wore many different occupational hats. Besides doing what we today would think of as philosophy, they also did physics, biology, mathematics, logic, and psychology. Their contributions to each of these fields were significant, but the Stoics' contribution to psychology is particularly impressive; indeed, the Stoic test strategy is based on their appreciation of a phenomenon that has been rediscovered by modern psychologists, who christened it the *framing effect*: how we mentally characterize a situation has a profound impact on how we respond to it emotionally.

The Stoics realized that we have considerable flexibility in how we frame the situations we experience. They discovered, more precisely, that by thinking of setbacks as tests of our character, we can dramatically alter our emotional response to them. We can, in particular, develop our ability to stay calm, even in the face of very significant setbacks, and this in turn can have a dramatic impact on our quality of life.

Many people, I should add, have an incorrect perception of the Stoics. They think of them as emotionless beings whose primary goal was to stand there and grimly take whatever life threw at them, but this was not the case. Their goal wasn't to banish *emotion* but to minimize the number of *negative* emotions— such as feelings of frustration, anger, grief, and envy—that they experienced. They had nothing against the experience of *positive* emotions, including delight and even joy.

We should think of the Stoics not as grim individuals but as eternal optimists who possessed a profound ability to put a positive spin on life's events. Rather than experiencing frustration and anger on being set back, they might experience no small measure of satisfaction on successfully dealing with the challenge presented them by that setback.

It is tempting, at this point, to describe the Stoics as patient people, and indeed they were, but a caveat is in order. In one sense, a *patient* person is one who can suffer a setback without complaint. This is not, however, what the Stoics were doing. Their goal was not to remain calm while *suffering* a setback but rather to experience a setback *without thereby suffering.* It is an important difference.

THIS BOOK IS AN EXERCISE in what might be thought of as twenty-first-century Stoicism. In these pages, I have fused the advice given by the first-century Stoic philosophers with the research done by late twentieth-century psychologists. Some in academia will resent me for meddling with classical Stoicism in this manner. They think of Stoicism the way they think of a priceless ancient relic—as something to be kept in a hermetically sealed case, to be seen but not touched. By contrast, I treat Stoicism as a tool that, although in need of sharpening because of the passage of time, is not only still useful but can have a profoundly beneficial impact on modern lives.

The ancient Stoics, I should add, probably wouldn't have objected to my "update" of their doctrines. Seneca in particular would have approved. It was he, after all, who declared, "I do not bind myself to some particular one of the Stoic masters.

I, too, have the right to form an opinion."[1] I do not claim to have the profound Stoic insights that Seneca possessed, but I do have available to me something he lacked—namely, the insight into the workings of the human mind gained by psychologists Amos Tversky and Daniel Kahneman, among others. I put these insights to work as I explore and explain the Stoic test strategy for dealing with setbacks.

I begin by describing the sorts of setbacks to which we are susceptible and the ways in which we typically respond to them. Although many people become frustrated, angry, anxious, or even despondent, others take setbacks in their stride. How do they do it? And can we emulate them?

I then explore the psychology of setbacks: why do they affect us emotionally the way they do? I go on to show how, instead of thinking of setbacks merely as unfortunate experiences, we can reframe them as tests of our resilience and ingenuity. Doing this can have a profound impact on how we respond to them. Instead of experiencing a mixture of anger and anxiety, we might be surprised to discover that we are rising enthusiastically to the challenge presented by a setback.

And finally I show how using the Stoic test strategy, besides helping our days go better, can help us have a good life—and when it comes time to make our exit from this world, a good death.

PART I

❮◉◉◉❯

DEALING WITH
LIFE'S CHALLENGES

CHAPTER 1

SETBACKS

When Things Take a Turn for the Worse

Sometimes your life is going along smoothly—splendidly, even—and then out of the blue, an obstacle appears. It can happen at work, at play, at home, or as was the case with my airport setback, while traveling. The plan you devised for yourself can no longer be carried out, so you have to come up with a new one.

In a typical day, you likely experience any number of setbacks. You might stub your toe or burn the toast you are making for breakfast. You might get caught in the rain without an umbrella or find yourself stuck in a traffic jam that makes you late for work. But these are low-grade setbacks, mere nuisances, hiccups in your daily routine. Getting the flu is a more significant setback, especially if it disrupts your plans for the next few days. Unexpectedly losing your job almost certainly counts as a major setback, inasmuch as it will force you to change many of your plans for the coming months. These setbacks are easily topped, though, by the death of a spouse, by discovering that you have a fatal illness, or by being imprisoned for a crime you didn't commit—or for one you did.

You might assume that your death would count as a major setback, but whether it does depends on what happens after you die. Suppose there is no life after death. Then your death might count as a setback for your survivors but not for you. After all, in the absence of an afterlife, dying requires no change of plans on your part; it instead means the end of planning, period.

If there is an afterlife, though, death might count as a setback. If reincarnation is true, you might come back as a person, in which case your death means another lifetime of dealing with setbacks, which itself might be construed as a major setback. And if you come back not as a person but as, say, a mosquito, you will face a whole new set of challenges—although you probably won't have sufficient brainpower to think of them as setbacks.

Suppose, however, that life after death involves not reincarnation into another body but continued existence as yourself. If you spend your afterlife in hell, then your death would represent the biggest setback imaginable. If you spend it in heaven, your death would represent not a setback but a major advance—a *setforward*, as it were—since it would involve a transition to an infinitely preferable existence.

It isn't clear, though, that you would be eternally happy in heaven. The problem is that when you went there, you would take your personality with you—including, quite likely, a propensity to take whatever you have for granted. Before long, you would start taking heaven's perfection for granted, and it would therefore cease to delight you. Perhaps God, in his infinite wisdom, will cause you to experience minor setbacks in heaven, just to prevent you from getting spoiled.

Along similar lines, Satan—if he exists—probably realizes that a hell in which setbacks are possible is more hellish than one in which they aren't. He will therefore take steps to prevent the damned from thinking their situation is hopeless. In particular, he might periodically allow them to experience a ray of hope, just so he can subsequently deal them a setback by cruelly extinguishing it.

SOMETIMES IT IS NATURE that sets you back. A deer might run into the path of your car, causing you to total it. Or a storm might leave you without electrical power for a week. During that time, you will discover the extent to which you take the presence of electricity for granted, and after power is restored, you will likely, if you are paying attention, discover how little time it takes you to start taking it for granted again.

In most cases, though, it isn't nature that obstructs your progress; it is other people. Often they do so without intending to harm you. An incompetent waiter, for example, might get your order mixed up. Or a driver might swerve to miss a deer, thereby avoiding a setback for himself but causing you to swerve and subsequently crash your car, thereby setting you back financially and maybe medically as well.

In other cases, someone sets you back on purpose. In order to punish his teenage daughter for getting bad grades, a father might take away her driving privileges for a month. To her, this might seem like one of the worst setbacks imaginable. Likewise, someone might set you back by picking your pocket. It is possible that he picked it because his money was stolen during a drug deal, in which case what to you counts as a setback will for him count as the workaround for a setback. Cases like this, by the way, show that setbacks can be contagious, much as diseases are. And finally, sheer malice might cause someone to set another person back: when you were a child, you might have deprived a sibling of a favorite toy, just to have the pleasure of watching him cry.

When you are angry that someone has set you back, it is helpful to recall that although other people are responsible for many of the setbacks you experience, you are likewise responsible for many of theirs. Yes, you find them annoying, but maybe, just maybe, they find you annoying as well. In particular, they may be annoyed by how easily annoyed you are. This fact is easy to forget, given that you are more acutely aware of the problems others cause you than you are of the problems you cause them. One sign of maturity is a realization of the extent to which you, either intentionally or unintentionally, make life difficult for those around you. Consequently, you should keep in mind the words of Seneca: "we are bad men living among bad men; and only one thing can calm us—we must agree to go easy on one another."[1]

Another thing to keep in mind about the setbacks you experience is that if you drew up a list of the people who have caused you setbacks, you would have to put yourself on that list, probably at the top. Many of the setbacks you experience are the result of poor planning on your part. You ran out of gas because you failed to check your car's fuel gauge before setting out on a trip. Or maybe you overslept on the last day of your vacation and missed your flight home because you failed to set your alarm. In other cases, you might be set back because of poor choices you made. You might, for example, develop a case of shingles because you refused to get vaccinated.

SETBACKS AND DESIRES ARE INTERCONNECTED: whether something counts as a setback depends on what a person wants, and how significant the setback is depends on how much he wants it. For many people, catching a cold is merely an annoyance, but for a marathoner who has trained for years to compete in the Olympics, catching a cold the day before the race will count as a major setback. Along similar lines, if you lose your two front teeth when you are a six-year-old, you will likely regard it not as a setback but as a rite of passage, as well as an opportunity to get a reward from the Tooth Fairy. Lose your front teeth the morning of your wedding, though, and you will almost certainly regard it as a disaster.

Because of the connection between setbacks and desires, if a person were incapable of experiencing desire, nothing would count as a setback. Conversely, to a person who has to have everything just so, setbacks will be routine occurrences in what is probably a very unhappy existence. Furthermore, a person with unusual desires will be subject to unusual setbacks. Most drowning people would be grateful if a good Samaritan pulled them from the water, but for someone trying to commit suicide, it would count as a setback.

How many setbacks you experience depends, as I have suggested, on how much foresight you possess. The days of a thoughtless person are likely to be filled with obstacles that he failed to anticipate, and as a result, he is likely to find life both frustrating and unfair. Were he not so thoughtless, he would fathom the reason for his misfortune.

Thoughtful people, by contrast, minimize the number of setbacks they experience by learning how the world works and using this knowledge to plan their activities. No matter how carefully they plan for the future, though, life will occasionally deal them a setback: the computer of their fully fueled and recently serviced hybrid vehicle might develop a glitch, thereby bringing it to a halt during rush hour on the freeway.

If you are reading these words, you are doubtless a thoughtful individual who spends time and energy thinking ahead in order to prevent foreseeable setbacks. But have you also spent time and energy developing a strategy for minimizing the emotional harm done to you by unforeseeable setbacks? You should have, since when you add up the costs imposed on you by being set back, you will often find that *the biggest cost by far is the emotional distress a setback triggers.*

You can gain important insight into setbacks by monitoring the impact they have on your life. Try keeping a setback journal in which you record the setbacks you experience, their source, their significance, and your response to them. Doing this will make you aware of the extent to which setbacks carry a double cost. The first might be described as their *physical* cost. If your car breaks down on the freeway, there are lots of things you will physically have to do, including spend money, to deal with this setback. Likewise, if your doctor tells you that you have cancer, the therapy you undergo will have physical costs in terms of sickness and discomfort.

But alongside these physical costs, there will be *emotional* costs. You might become very angry as the result of the car breakdown, and you might become profoundly sad as the result of the cancer diagnosis. Not only that, but in many cases, the emotional cost of a setback is far greater than the physical cost. Wouldn't it be great if you could reduce the emotional cost of a setback or even eliminate it entirely? It turns out that you can, by using the Stoic test strategy.

WE CAN LEARN A LOT from studying other people's responses to setbacks. Such study is facilitated by people's willingness to share their setback stories. Sometimes the simple act of greeting someone—"How are things going?"—will trigger one. Likewise, your comment to a friend that your water heater sprang a leak might elicit a reciprocal setback tale: "So did mine, last year."

People are also inclined to top whatever setback tales we share with them. When we tell them that we got sick after eating at a restaurant, they might respond by telling us, in considerable detail, about the time they were sick for three days after eating at a taco stand in Tijuana, Mexico. There are also people who don't just mention setbacks they have experienced but talk about them almost exclusively, and in the process they rejuvenate the anger triggered in them by those setbacks. Such individuals, needless to say, are not the most agreeable of companions. Nevertheless, when you encounter them, you should pay close attention. Do you sometimes respond to setbacks the way they do? And if so, is there a way for you to overcome this tendency? If you can, your days will go much smoother, and you might, as a result, find that you are enjoying your life as never before.

Sometimes we share our setback stories as a kind of public service. We hope that by telling others about a setback, we can warn them of an obstacle that they, too, might encounter. And by telling people how we responded to that setback, we can help them deal with it if, despite our warning, they fall victim to it. In other cases, people who tell us about a setback want our help: consider the stranger who tells us her purse was snatched, leaving her without any cash, credit cards, or ID. In yet other cases, someone will tell us a setback story in the hope that we will join them in their fight against the social injustice that gave rise to that setback.

People also tell setback stories in an attempt to impress us with their resilience in the face of setbacks and their ingenuity in finding workarounds for them. Others have the opposite motiva-tion for telling setback stories: they seek not our admiration but our pity. They might, in particular, want us to reassure them that it isn't their fault that they experienced the setback they did—an unfair world is instead to blame.

WATCHING PEOPLE BEING SET BACK can be deliciously rewarding—if, at any rate, we think they deserve to be set back. Suppose, for example, that your abusive boss is summarily fired by his boss. Justice at last! Watching people overcome setbacks can also be entertaining. This is one of the reasons people have an interest in spectator sports. We love to see the team we are root-ing for impose setbacks on opposing teams. In baseball, batters are struck out, players are injured, and games are lost. We also love watching our favored team recover, in heroic fashion, from a setback it experienced. Remove the setbacks from sports, and they would become as boring as watching someone mow a lawn.

When we aren't watching sports, we might spend our time reading a novel. Our interest in literature can also be explained, in part, by our fascination with setbacks. Novels are full of them, and with good reason. A novel in which two characters fall in love on their first meeting, get married, never fight, and live hap-pily ever after would be a commercial failure. Authors realize this and therefore go out of their way to confront characters with obstacles. As a result, their characters' relationships don't run smoothly: hearts get broken. Their lives are also filled with drama: they might contract an illness or be the victim of a crime. The same rule applies to cinema.

Most people don't attempt to write short stories, novels, or screenplays, thinking it would require a degree of creativity that they lack. Ask them to describe a recent setback, though, and you might trigger their creative juices. They might add elements and characters to their setback tale in an attempt to make the setback sound less foreseeable and more challenging than it was. By doing this, they make their solution to the setback seem all the more amazing—or if they failed to find a solution, they make the failure more understandable.

Another time our creative juices flow is when we are asleep. We dream about strange things, some good and some bad, and one thing that makes bad dreams bad is the setbacks we experience in them. We might be unable to find things we need, be prevented from seeing people we need to see, or be unable to do things we need to do, such as shout out a word of warning to a loved one who is in imminent danger. A single dream might contain a chain of setbacks: just when we think we have found a solution to one, another setback prevents us from implementing that solution. *Drat!* When our dreaming selves finally conclude that a setback is insurmountable—suppose the dragon that has been blocking our path through the woods has laid its reptilian claws on us—we often respond by waking up. And on doing so, we will likely feel compelled to share our dream-world setbacks with friends and relatives.

The setbacks we experience while awake cannot likewise be

eliminated simply by opening our eyes. It is therefore important that we develop an effective strategy for dealing with them. Unfortunately, the strategy that many people employ isn't just ineffective, it's counterproductive. It results in them becoming first frustrated and then angry, which substantially increases the harm done them by the setback.

CHAPTER 2

ANGER ISSUES

Different people respond to setbacks in different ways. Some people are quite sensitive to them: even a minor setback will have a significant impact on their emotional state, and after experiencing it, they won't bounce back quickly. They might feel incapable of finding a workaround for the setback, or they might play the role of victim and complain to anyone who will listen how unfair it is that they were set back in this manner. They might go on to argue that because of their victimization, they shouldn't have to come up with a workaround; someone else should have to do it for them.

Most of us, though, are tougher than this. We respond to the setbacks we experience not by feeling helpless and defeated but by feeling frustrated. In many cases, this response is involuntary: we no more choose to get frustrated in the face of a setback than a hay fever sufferer chooses to sneeze when pollen is in the air. It's just what we do.

There is, however, an important difference between sneezing and getting frustrated. Sneezing removes whatever is irritating our sinuses and thereby makes us feel better. Getting frustrated, on the other hand, often begets anger. This is unfortunate, since anger is incompatible with happiness; indeed, anger can be thought of as anti-joy. Consequently, getting frustrated in response to a setback only makes things worse.

Unfortunately, any anger we experience is likely to be contagious. This is because we often direct our setback-triggered anger at someone, and when we express our anger to that person, he or she could very well respond by returning it. In other cases, we share our anger not with the person who made us angry but with an innocent bystander. We do this in part because we seek to validate our anger: we want this person to assure us that we have every reason to be angry. Better still, we want this person to commiserate with us. The word *commiserate* comes from the Latin *commiseratus*, which in turn derives from *com*, meaning "with," and *miser*, meaning "wretched." We want them, in other words, to get angry as well, so they can share our wretchedness. Of course, if it was foolish for one person to get angry about something, it is twice as foolish for two people to do so, especially if the second person isn't directly affected by whatever it was that made the first person angry.

Along these lines, suppose that after I experience a setback, a friend tells me that she feels bad about it. Maybe she doesn't *literally* feel bad—all she's trying to say is that she wishes I hadn't been set back. This behavior would be perfectly understandable. Suppose, however, that she *literally does* feel bad; suppose, in particular, that she is angry or sad about my having been set back. This is the last thing a Stoic like myself would want. I might ask a friend for advice on finding a workaround for a setback, but I would never ask—or expect—a friend to be angry or sad about my being set back. This sort of commiseration turns a setback for one person into a setback for two, without helping the first person overcome the setback. In other words, it only makes matters worse.

WHEN WE BECOME ANGRY, we have two options: we can either express our anger or suppress it. If suppressed, our anger might take root in us and enter a kind of dormant state, only to spring back to life at an inopportune moment: a year after experiencing a setback that angered us, our anger might flare into our consciousness again. Furthermore, these anger flashbacks can continue for decades. As people age, they forget a lot, but they cling to old wrongs that were done them. A ninety-year-old woman, who doesn't know what day of the week or even what year it is, might nevertheless be able to recount, in a fair amount of detail and with renewed ire, an incident that upset her half a century before.

Suppose that instead of suppressing our anger, we express it. Do so in a manner that breaks the law, and we might end up in prison. And while expressing anger in a socially acceptable manner may or may not hurt the person at whom we are angry, it is certain to have a negative impact on ourselves.

There are angry people who, when you try to calm them down, respond by saying that they have every right to be angry. If you point out that their anger is making them miserable, they might respond by saying, with some indignation, that they have every right to be miserable. If you then question the value of such a right, they might back off a bit and say that what they mean is that it is perfectly understandable that they would be miserable, given what they have been through. Yes, it is understandable, but it is nevertheless unfortunate. And wouldn't it be tragic if they went through life needlessly miserable as the result of routinely experiencing anger that they could have avoided?

The Stoic philosopher Seneca understood how much harm we do by allowing ourselves to get angry. In his essay "On Anger," he asserts, "No plague has cost the human race more."[1] Because of anger, people insult and sue each other, they divorce each other, and they hit and even kill each other. Because of anger, the nations those people live in go to war, and as a result, millions might die at the hands of people they have never even met. Cities might be reduced to rubble, and civilizations might fall.

SO WHAT SHOULD WE DO when we feel that someone has wronged us? Our first objective, says Seneca, should be to avoid getting angry. That way we will have no anger to deal with and therefore no anger either to express or to suppress. Lots of people will immediately dismiss this advice. We don't have it in our power *not* to get angry, they will explain; it's just what people do.

I would argue to the contrary. Although I would not describe myself as an angry person, I am certainly capable of anger, but the role it plays in my life has changed as a result of studying Stoic philosophy.

My epiphany regarding anger came at a doctor's office. It is my custom to bring along reading material to medical appointments, since doctors are so often late. On this day I had brought—what else?—Seneca's essay on anger. The doctor ended up being an hour late, and during that hour, I made an interesting discovery: although I knew full well that I had every right to be angry at her for making me wait, I just couldn't bring myself to do so. Seneca had me convinced that it would be a foolish thing to do—that by getting angry, I would only be hurting myself. This incident demonstrated the possibility of thinking my way out of becoming angry, something I had previously thought was impossible.

As a result of this epiphany, I started paying attention to the role anger played in my life. In traffic jams, I watched myself yell at the drivers of other cars. They couldn't hear me, though, and even if they could, they were as stuck as I was and therefore could do little other than what they were doing. So why yell? Wasn't it because yelling made me feel better? It might indeed have done so, but only for a moment. Then my anger would rise again. I would have been far better off, I told myself, not to have gotten angry in the first place; then I wouldn't have felt a need to do something to make myself feel better—temporarily.

As I continued my investigation of anger, I gathered additional evidence of the harm I did myself by getting angry. I found myself, for example, yelling at the politicians I saw on television. Wasn't this foolish behavior, inasmuch as they couldn't hear me? I also watched as anger I had experienced in the past rekindled within me. I would be just about to fall asleep when some wrong done to me months before would drift into my mind. I would then toss and turn for a few hours and wake up crabby the next day.

As a result of this investigation, I found myself getting angry about my tendency to get angry about foolish things. It was time, I decided, to deal with my anger issues. In particular, if I could learn how not to get angry about the setbacks I experienced in everyday life, there wouldn't be much anger left to deal with.

At this point, I could have done the obvious thing and started seeing an anger management therapist. Because of my exposure to the Stoics, though, I knew another option was available to me: I could take a closer look at Stoic advice on anger management and experiment with it. What I have found is that this advice has not lost its effectiveness in the two millennia since it was first promulgated. That is why I am sharing it with readers.

CHAPTER 3

RESILIENCE

We might pity those who are broken or incapacitated by life's setbacks. Theirs cannot be a happy existence. We might also sympathize with those who respond to setbacks with frustration and anger. It is such a common response that we might have concluded that it is, for us humans, the default response. Look around us, though, and we can find individuals who quickly bounce back from a setback—or better still, who don't need to bounce, since they don't get upset to begin with. Such individuals come off looking strong and even heroic.

The astronaut Neil Armstrong was one of them. He had been chosen to pilot the lunar excursion module on the Apollo 11 moon mission. This was the vehicle that would land on the moon's surface while the command module remained in orbit. To perfect his landing technique, Armstrong practiced by flying a lunar lander trainer here on Earth. This ungainly vehicle consisted of a central rocket to provide lift, surrounded by side-pointing thrusters to provide stability. Flying it was likened to trying to balance a dinner plate on the end of a broom handle.

Armstrong had flown the vehicle successfully many times, but on May 6, 1968, a thruster stuck, meaning that he lost control. The craft started tilting erratically, and finally, when it was just about to turn upside down, Armstrong ejected. Two seconds later the vehicle crashed and was instantly engulfed in a fireball. Other than biting his tongue at the end of his parachute-assisted landing, Armstrong walked away unscathed.[1]

A few hours after the crash, another astronaut, Alan Bean, encountered Armstrong, still in his flight suit and doing paperwork. He exchanged pleasantries with Armstrong and went on his way. Only then did someone tell him what had happened. In a state of disbelief, Bean went back to Armstrong's office to ask whether he had indeed crashed the lander. "Yeah," Armstrong responded. "I did." Pressed for details, Armstrong explained that "I lost control and had to bail out of the darn thing." And that was all he had to say.

Bean subsequently commented that if another astronaut had survived a crash landing, he would have made a big deal of it. He wouldn't have complained, but if he survived, he would have boasted of his piloting skills:

I don't think it was that Neil was so extraordinarily cooler than the other guys. But offhand, I can't think of another person, let alone another astronaut, who would have just gone back to his office after ejecting a fraction of a second before getting killed. He never got up at an all-pilots meeting and told us anything about it. That was an incident that colored my opinion about Neil ever since. He was so different than other people.[2]

It turns out that Armstrong, although unusual, is by no means unique. Look around, and we can find other examples of people who have demonstrated the ability to rise, quietly and bravely, to the challenges presented by significant setbacks.

EARLY ON THE MORNING of October 31, 2003, thirteen-year-old Bethany Hamilton went surfing off the coast of Kauai, one of the Hawaiian Islands. She was accompanied by her best friend, Alana Blanchard, along with Alana's father and brother.[3] The water was calm, so they relaxed on their boards, hoping the surf would build. Hamilton's right hand was holding the tip of her board, while her left arm dangled in the cool water. Then without warning, there was a flash of gray. Before she could comprehend what was happening, a shark bit off her left arm, just below the shoulder. In an instant, the water turned bright red. Strangely, because the injury was so severe, Hamilton experienced little pain. She did her best to stay calm and started paddling toward shore with her remaining arm.

With the help of her fellow surfers, she made it to the shore and was rushed to the hospital. By the time they got there, she had lost an estimated 60 percent of her blood and was very close to dead. Through a remarkable coincidence, her father was already at the hospital. He had been scheduled to have knee surgery that morning and was on the operating table when a nurse came in and said he would have to leave in order to make room for an incoming shark attack victim, a thirteen-year-old girl. He knew the local surfing community well enough to guess that the girl was either his daughter Bethany or her friend Alana. A few minutes later he was informed that it was indeed his daughter.

Hamilton had started surfing as a child, and by age seven, she could catch and ride waves without assistance from her parents. Not long thereafter, she won the first surfing competition she entered. By the time she was thirteen, she not only had won dozens of trophies but also had a sponsor. Her goal, before the attack, had been to become a pro surfer.

As Hamilton lay in the hospital recovering, she considered her options. She concluded that her surfing days were over: how can you surf with only one arm? Perhaps she would become a surf photographer, or maybe she would switch to soccer, a sport in which arms play a minor role. Shortly thereafter, though, she decided it was too early to give up on surfing. Her doctor was encouraging. He explained that although the list of things she would have to *do differently* was very long, the list of things she *couldn't do* was short. He gave her permission to give surfing another try, as long as she waited until her stitches were out.

During her recovery, Hamilton became aware of all the obstacles she would have to surmount in order to get her life back on track. How, she wondered, do you button a shirt or tie your shoes with only one hand? And how do you peel an orange? With a bit of research and experimentation, she was able to find workarounds. She stocked her wardrobe with buttonless tops and with shoes that didn't need to be tied. The trick to peeling an orange with only one hand, she discovered, was to hold it with your feet. She moved on to confront what for her was a rather more significant challenge: how can you surf with only one arm?

On the day before Thanksgiving—only twenty-six days after the attack—Hamilton gave surfing a try and quickly made some important discoveries. The first was that she would have to modify the paddling technique she used to get her board out where the waves were. The second was that she would have to change the way she moved from a prone position to a standing position on the board. Most surfers, including Hamilton before the attack, put their hands palm down on the board next to their ribs and then push their abdomen up. She experimented and found that she could place her one hand in the center of the board and push. Once up, she found it wasn't too hard to balance using only one arm. After a few falls, she successfully rode a wave and thereby silenced the voice of doubt in her mind that had insisted she would never surf again. She celebrated this triumph by shedding tears of joy.

Hamilton subsequently returned to competitive surfing and in 2005, less than two years after the attack, won the National Scholastic Surfing Association National Championship. Shortly thereafter, she turned pro, winning the first contest she entered and many more after that. She also became a media sensation, appearing on *20/20*, *Inside Edition*, and *Oprah*. She was okay with all this attention, since it gave her a platform for sharing with others her belief in God. It also allowed her to act as role model for those who, like herself, had experienced significant setbacks.

◉

BETHANY HAMILTON WAS ATTACKED by a shark. Alison Botha, a twenty-seven-year-old living in South Africa, was attacked by two men.[4] Late on the night of December 18, 1994, she was parking her car near her home when a man reached through the open window and put a knife to her throat. He ordered her to move to the passenger seat, then got into the car and drove them away. Shortly thereafter he picked up a second man, and they drove into the countryside.

The car came to a stop at a deserted spot. One of the men raped her and then, after a pause, savagely attacked her, stabbing her thirty-seven times in the abdomen and pubic region, and slashing her throat seventeen times. The two men then drove off, leaving her for dead—except that she wasn't. In a stunned state, Botha dragged herself to the road, where she would have a better chance of getting help. Doing so was difficult because her windpipe had been severed and her intestines were falling out of her abdomen.

One car came along, but when the driver saw her naked, bloody body, it just kept going. Fortunately for Botha, the next car did stop. A young man named Tiaan Eilerd called for an ambulance and did his best to stanch the bleeding. When the ambulance finally arrived at the hospital—more than two hours later—the medical personnel there were astonished by the brutality of the attack. They were also amazed that she was still alive. Police were subsequently able to track down Botha's attackers, who were tried, found guilty, and given lengthy prison sentences.

Botha's recovery was long and painful, and during it, she became depressed. Things turned around, though, when she got an invitation to tell her story to an audience. She discovered that by sharing this story, she could make a positive difference in the lives of other people, many of whom had themselves experienced major or even traumatic setbacks. Before long, she was in demand as an inspirational speaker.

In her talks, she described the philosophy by which she lives: "We cannot always control what happens in our life . . . , but we can always control what we do with what happens."[5] It is a strategy that Stoic philosopher Epictetus would have applauded. Botha had come to realize that she had it in her power to choose whether to respond to the attack with anger, and she thereupon decided not to, knowing that anger has the power to devour those who experience it.

Botha subsequently married, and nine years after the attack, much to her surprise, she got pregnant. Her doctors had assumed that the wounds to her abdomen had destroyed her reproductive system, making biological motherhood impossible, but this turned out not to be the case. Tiaan Eilerd, the man who had rescued her after her assault, was there in the delivery room. His earlier encounter with Botha had inspired him to go into medicine, and he was now a doctor.

ROGER EBERT WAS MOVIE CRITIC for the *Chicago Sun-Times* from 1967 until his death in 2013. In 1975, he also became cohost of PBS's *Sneak Previews* show. He was thriving, both professionally and personally. And then in 2002, he was diagnosed with salivary cancer. He was treated for it, but the cancer returned. Doctors treated it again, and things were looking hopeful, but then his carotid artery burst. He barely survived the episode. It subsequently ruptured six more times. In the end, as a result of all these ruptures, all the cancer, and all the surgery, Ebert lost the ability to speak. Not only that, but the reconstructive surgery done on his jaw left him looking like a caricature. His face had a permanent, cartoon-like grin, with its mouth hanging open.

In March 2011, Ebert gave a TED Talk.[6] More precisely, he sat in silence on the stage while a computerized speech synthesizer read from a script he had previously prepared. After a minute, his wife and some friends started similarly speaking on his behalf. (Ebert had worried that if his computer did the entire talk, people would be lulled to sleep by its voice.) While the others read his words, Ebert used gestures to make jokes, usually at his own expense. The audience at first was unsure how to react but soon figured out that although Ebert had lost his ability to speak, he had not lost his sense of humor. They laughed, and when the talk was over, they gave him a standing ovation. It was a remarkable and touching performance, and in giving it, what courage Ebert had displayed! He died two years later, at age seventy.

Watching the video of Ebert's talk reminded me how easy it is for us to take our abilities for granted. At some point in his decline, Ebert must have uttered his last words, but in his lecture he said he couldn't remember what they were. This, however, is understandable. All his life, he could safely assume that the words he spoke would be followed by other words, so he had no need to remember them. This time turned out to be different, though.

It struck me that I, too, will someday utter my last words; indeed, there is a long-shot chance that I have already uttered them. More generally, for everything I do, there will be a last time I do it. You might think these are dark and depressing thoughts, but they can have just the opposite effect. They can help us transform our ability to speak from something we take completely for granted into what it in fact is—something remarkable and precious.

Many, on hearing Ebert's story, would use the word *unlucky* to describe him, but a much more fitting word would be *unvanquished*. During the last decade of his life, he experienced enough setbacks for several lifetimes and yet was not embittered by his fate. It was a triumph of the human spirit.

WHEREAS EBERT HAD LOST his ability to speak, many others have lost their ability to move. Lou Gehrig was one of the greatest baseball players ever to live. During the twelve seasons between 1926 and 1937, he batted .300 or above, and in 1934 he batted a remarkable .363. In the 1938 season, he fell off this pace a bit and batted "only" .295. He complained about feeling tired. When he showed up for spring training in 1939, he had clearly lost his coordination and power. This was visible in his hitting and base running, as well as in his muddled attempts to catch the ball.

Sports writers speculated about what had happened to him. His coaches considered benching him, but their respect for him made this impossible. Finally, on May 2, 1939, Gehrig benched himself "for the good of the team." When the stadium announcer told the fans that Gehrig would not be playing in that day's game, ending his record of appearing in 2,130 consecutive games, the audience gave him a standing ovation. Meanwhile Gehrig sat in the dugout, teary-eyed.

On June 19, his thirty-sixth birthday, Gehrig was diagnosed with amyotrophic lateral sclerosis—commonly known as ALS or Lou Gehrig's disease—and on June 21 the Yankees announced his retirement. On July 4, which had been proclaimed Lou Gehrig Appreciation Day, Gehrig gave his famous farewell speech: "For the past two weeks you have been reading about the bad break I got. Yet today I consider myself the luckiest man on the face of the earth." He went on to thank his fans, his fellow players, his coach, the groundskeepers, his mother-in-law (who sided with him in squabbles with her own daughter), his parents (who educated him and gave him a strong body), and his wife (who showed "more courage than you dreamed existed"). "I might have been given a bad break," he concluded, "but I've got an awful lot to live for."[7]

And Gehrig did live on for another two years. During that time, he experienced setback after setback, as abilities were stripped from him. He later wrote that "I intend to hold on as long as possible and then if the inevitable comes, I will accept it philosophically and hope for the best. That's all we can do." Although there is no evidence that Gehrig had read the Stoics, he appears to have been a fine example of what I call a *congenital Stoic*: he seems to have known instinctively what the Stoic philosophers had figured out two thousand years earlier.

THE THEORETICAL PHYSICIST STEPHEN HAWKING was afflicted by Lou Gehrig's disease in 1963, at age twenty-one. Like Gehrig, he had to watch ability after ability disappear. When he could no longer walk, he got around at first in a regular wheelchair and then in a motorized wheelchair that he could steer by moving a joystick with his fingers. When he could no longer control his hand, he steered with his cheek muscles. Early on, he could communicate by talking, but as years went by, his speech devolved into mumbling. Then a bout of pneumonia forced doctors to do a tracheotomy, which deprived him of even his mumbles. He overcame this setback by raising his eyebrows to pick out, with the aid of an assistant, letters on a card and thereby spell out words.

Because of his celebrity status in the world of science,

Hawking had lots of help in dealing with the setbacks he faced. His physicist friends put him in touch with engineers and programmers, who set up a system by which he could type computer messages using a clicker. This was enhanced by the addition of a speech synthesizer that could read those messages aloud. In 1997 Gordon Moore, cofounder of Intel, encountered Hawking at a conference and put his employees to work improving the setup Hawking was using. Other disabled individuals have benefited from the resulting technologies, so Hawking's setback had a silver lining for humanity. Many setbacks do, especially if the person set back is resilient.

Despite his disabilities, Hawking was able to do interviews and give lectures. In these events, it may have looked like what he said was coming directly from his brain, but this was an illusion. The sentences were all previously composed. When he "spoke," the computer was reading from a manuscript, one sentence at a time. Even though Hawking was British, the speech synthesizer he used, because of its American origins, had an American accent. It also sounded very robotic. Other, more sophisticated voices became available, but Hawking wisely stayed with the voice that had become, as far as the world was concerned, *his* voice.

Gehrig's setback was in various respects more challenging than Hawking's. Because he was a gifted athlete, Gehrig's physical abilities lay at the core of his self-concept. By losing these abilities, he was losing an important part of his identity. Hawking's self-identity, by contrast, centered on his mental abilities, and he retained them despite the deterioration of his body. Also, Hawking benefited from technological breakthroughs that were unavailable to Gehrig. Nevertheless, both men bravely met a challenge that would have defeated many. That is why we admire them, even if we are indifferent to baseball and are clueless when it comes to the physics of black holes.

YOU MIGHT THINK THAT Gehrig and Hawking would represent worst-case scenarios, but you would be mistaken. Consider, in particular, those individuals who have locked-in syndrome. Although their minds are still active, they have lost all muscular control except, maybe, in their eyelids. And as medical setbacks go, this one is sudden. You are in the prime of life, going about your everyday business, when you start feeling strange. You pass out, and when you wake up, days or weeks later, you are in a hospital. You can still see and hear, but you can't move a muscle, meaning you can't ask questions. This is because you have experienced a stroke in your brain stem. It has severed communications between your brain and your body, without otherwise affecting that brain and body.

This is what happened to high school teacher Richard Marsh. He awoke in a hospital, attached to a respirator. His doctors, who assumed he was brain dead, felt free to have conversations about him in his presence. At one point, they told his wife that he had only a 2 percent chance of surviving, and that if he did survive, he would be a vegetable. Did she want them to turn off the ventilator? Richard Marsh screamed *no!*—internally, that is. He could not move any of his muscles, including the ones that would let him speak. Fortunately, his wife declined the offer, and as a result, Marsh walked out of the hospital four months after his stroke.[8]

As locked-in patients go, Marsh was lucky. Jean-Dominique Bauby, the forty-three-year-old editor-in-chief of French *Elle* magazine, had a brain stem stroke, and when he woke up in a hospital, he could not move any part of his body except for two things: he could slowly swivel his head, and he could blink his left eye. Because he could not blink his right eye, there was danger that its cornea would dry out and ulcerate. To prevent this from happening, doctors sewed shut the lids of that eye.

Bauby could not swallow, meaning he could not eat or drink anything, so he had to be fed through a tube that passed into his stomach. Imagine it: he could still smell french fries but could not eat them. He could remember the last meal he ate but knew he probably would never have that meal again—or any other meal, for that matter. His inability to swallow had another consequence. He could not do something that you do all day long, albeit unconsciously—namely, swallow the saliva that continually flows into your mouth. As a result, he tended to drool. It is easy, on encountering an immobile, speechless, one-eyed, drooling individual, to assume that he is a vegetable, but Bauby's mind was still fully functional. Indeed, despite his locked-in condition, he wrote the memoir *The Diving Bell and the Butterfly*, which was made into a 2007 movie of the same name.

He dictated the book with his left eye. Other people would recite the alphabet to him, and when they came to the letter he wanted, he would blink. He found that some people, rather than patiently going through the alphabet, would anticipate the letter or word he was trying to communicate, but this only slowed things down. A good translator would let him finish words and sentences. Because editing those sentences was such a laborious process, he carefully composed them in his mind before dictating them.

Bauby doesn't seem to have been a practicing Stoic before he became locked in. He did write, though, about "acquiring stoicism" as a mechanism for coping with his setback.[9] Unlike Marsh, Bauby did not walk out of the hospital. He died in 1997, fifteen months after his stroke—and two days after the French publication of his memoir.

Realize that Bauby's situation, although bad, could have been worse. Patients with *total* locked-in syndrome can't even move their eyelids, making it difficult for doctors to discover that their mind is still functioning, and if it is, making it impossible to communicate with them. But such cases have a ray of hope. Technological breakthroughs have made it possible for locked-in patients to communicate with thought alone. Electrodes implanted in their brain send signals to a computer. By this means, a patient can pick out letters on a computer screen. The process is very slow, though: one woman patient was able to "type" at the rate of one or two words per minute—and felt delighted to be able to do so.[10] I have found it useful, when my word processor is balky, to contemplate her predicament.

In his autobiography, Theodore Roosevelt offered this bit of Stoic-inspired advice: "Do what you can, with what you've got, where you are."[11] This is precisely what the locked-in individuals I have described did. They were thereby able to transform what might otherwise have been characterized as tragic lives into lives that were both courageous and admirable.

AS ONE LAST EXAMPLE OF RESILIENCE in the face of a setback, consider the case of the Stoic philosopher Paconius Agrippinus, who in around 67 CE was openly critical of Emperor Nero. A messenger came to inform him that he was being tried in the Senate. His response: "I hope it goes well, but it is time for me to exercise and bathe, so that is what I will do." Subsequently, another messenger appeared with the news that he had been found guilty of treasonous behavior and condemned. "To banishment or to death?" he asked. "To banishment," the messenger replied. Agrippinus responded with a question: "Was my estate at Aricia taken?" "No," said the messenger. "In that case," said Agrippinus, "I will go to Aricia and dine."[12]

In behaving in this manner, Agrippinus was simply applying advice that, although perfectly sensible, is easy to forget. When the number of options available is limited, it is foolish to fuss and fret. We should instead simply choose the best of them and get on with life. To behave otherwise is to waste precious time and energy.

Setback stories like those related above leave me with curiously mixed emotions. On hearing them, I might be moved to tears, but at the same time, I might feel ashamed of myself for taking so much of my life for granted. In the course of going about my daily business, I might experience a minor setback, like discovering that all the parking spaces close to the grocery store have been taken. *Oh, great!* I might think, only to recall that in walking the few more steps that I was complaining about, I was living the life that Stephen Hawking or Jean-Dominique Bauby could only dream of. Shame on me!

Although setback stories can sadden and shame us, they can also be enormously uplifting. In them, we encounter ordinary people who have experienced setbacks vastly more challenging than any we are likely to experience, and who, instead of wallowing in self-pity, responded with courage and intelligence. They thereby transformed what could have been personal tragedy into personal triumph.

CHAPTER 4

CAN WE BECOME
MORE RESILIENT?

In the preceding chapters, we explored what might be called the *resilience continuum*. At one end we find resilient individuals. When they encounter a setback, they bounce back quickly—or better still, they don't get upset by the setback, meaning they have nothing to bounce back from. They come off looking strong and even heroic. At the other end of the continuum we find fragile individuals. On being set back, they become flustered, angry, or even despondent. As a result, they tend to be unhappy, and their friends and relatives may pity them rather than admire them.

Why isn't everyone resilient? The easy and popular answer: because not everyone can be. It is one of those things, like eye color, that we can't control. It is to a large extent a consequence of how we happen to be "wired." Some people are lucky enough to be born resilient; others are not.

But this answer is mistaken. If people were "born resilient," the way they are born with a certain eye color, we would expect resilience to be fairly constant from generation to generation, the way eye color is. If two parents have brown eyes, their children quite likely will. Recent history indicates, however, that this is not the case with resilience.

Consider London during the Second World War. It was subjected to regular bombings. Before the war, experts had predicted that those who were bombed would experience extreme distress and that morale would be crushed. This is one reason Hitler thought it was worth doing. But just the opposite happened. People took to heart the advice to "Keep calm and carry on." They followed in the footsteps of their British ancestors and kept, to the best of their ability, a stiff upper lip.

In the last seventy years, though, things have changed. The great-grandchildren of these individuals are in many cases substantially less resilient than their ancestors were. And if this is true in Britain, it is arguably even truer in the United States. How can this be the case? What happened?

Like any social change, this one is a complex phenomenon with lots of causal factors. One of them is arguably the 1969 publication of *On Death and Dying*. In this best-selling book, Elisabeth Kübler-Ross described the five stages of grief: denial, anger, bargaining, depression, and finally, acceptance. These were the stages, she said, that those diagnosed with a terminal illness typically go through—and the stages that these individuals *should* go through to effectively deal with grief.

She later broadened her theory of grief recovery to include

other setbacks, such as the death of a relative, the loss of a spouse through divorce, and even the loss of a job. The public took her recommendations to heart and concluded that it was risky to deal with setbacks on their own. This and other factors triggered a boom in psychological counseling, and by the end of the century, when a disaster struck, busloads of counselors would descend on ground zero to help its survivors.

PSYCHOLOGISTS WEREN'T ALONE in undermining people's resilience. Politicians also got into the act. Voters were not responsible, they said, for many of the setbacks they experienced. Those setbacks were instead inflicted on them by the unfair and imperfect society in which they lived. The politicians' message: "Bad and stupid people have set you back. Vote for me, and I will make things right."

Politicians are, to be sure, correct in thinking that people can be the targets of injustice. They are also correct in thinking that many of the setbacks people experience are the result of that mistreatment. Politicians have an unfortunate habit, though, of thinking of these people and referring to them not as *targets* of injustice but as its *victims*. It is a label that many people are quick to accept. Being a victim, after all, relieves you of responsibility for many of the aspects of your life that have gone wrong. It also entitles you to special treatment: victims need time and space in which to recover and maybe even some kind of monetary compensation. At the same time, though, playing the role of victim is likely to increase the anguish you experience as the result of the wrongs that are done you. You will feel emotionally helpless.

A resilient person will refuse to play the role of victim. To play this role is to invite pity, and she doesn't regard herself as a pitiful being. She is strong and capable. She may not be able to control whether she is a target of injustice, but she has considerable control over how she responds to being targeted. She can let it ruin her day and possibly her life, or she can respond to it bravely, remaining upbeat while she looks for workarounds to the obstacles that people have wrongly placed in her path.

This may sound naïve, but it describes the way many of the ancient Stoics responded to injustice. They tended to say and do things that got them into trouble with the powers that be. This was the case, as we have seen, with Paconius Agrippinus. It was also the case with other first-century philosophers, including Thrasea Paetus, Rubellius Plautus, Barea Soranus, and their Stoic teacher, Musonius Rufus. These individuals were remarkable for the courage they demonstrated in the face of the setbacks they experienced.

Musonius Rufus was banished not once but twice, the second time to Gyaros, a desolate island in the Aegean Sea. He did not respond by becoming depressed or despondent, and he didn't complain about his situation to those who visited him. In a lecture he subsequently gave, Musonius pointed out that exile does not deprive us of the things that matter most. An exiled person is not prevented from having courage, self-control, wisdom, or any other virtue.[1] Furthermore, it is possible to profit from exile. It transformed Diogenes of Sinope, for example, from an ordinary person into one of the most fascinating philosophers of the fourth century BCE.[2] Other people, whose bodies had been ruined by luxurious living, regained their health as the result of being banished.[3]

Consider how different our world would be if Nelson Mandela and Mahatma Gandhi had played the role of victim. Suppose, more precisely, that they had been raised to think it was emotionally risky to deal with setbacks on their own and that at any rate, they shouldn't have to deal with them. Under such circumstances, they probably wouldn't have responded to the injustice they experienced as bravely as they did. They might instead have made an appointment with a therapist for advice on how best to cope with their situation, or they might have restricted their efforts to writing heartfelt letters to elected officials.

BY THE END OF THE TWENTIETH CENTURY, many adults were willing to play the role of victim. At the same time, many children were being raised to believe that they should not and could not, on their own, rise to the challenges that life would likely present.

On the advice of psychologists, parents of the 1990s and 2000s worked hard to give their children setback-free childhoods. They supervised their children's play to prevent mishaps, and when accidents nevertheless happened, they cleaned up the resulting messes rather than expecting their children to do so.

Likewise, when disputes arose among the children in their care, these parents assumed the role of referee instead of letting the children work things out for themselves.

These overly protective parents also took steps to prevent their children from experiencing failure. The theory seems to have been that children who experienced lots of success would get used to succeeding and would therefore be more likely to succeed in the future. As a result, there were no longer winners and losers in competitive events; instead, everyone was a winner, so everyone got a trophy. In many schools, there were no longer failing grades; everyone who showed up for an exam got a passing grade, and everyone who stuck around for four years of high school graduated.

When it came time for their children to apply for admission to college, their parents might have ghostwritten the "personal statement" required on their applications.[4] These helicopter parents, as they came to be known, might have been thrilled to see how high their children's grades were in the college courses they subsequently took. Whereas *they* might have worked hard for a gentleman's C, their offspring were capable of getting As and Bs with minimal effort. Surely it was evidence that their parenting strategies had succeeded. Wasn't it?[5]

Imagine the life of a person—let's call him John—whose childhood has few setbacks, thanks in large part to the efforts of the adults in his life. Although this sheltered childhood will be pleasant, it deprives John of the chance to develop his setback-response skills, a downside that might not become apparent until he leaves home.

When the adult John is set back, he might not rebound; he might instead experience a potent mix of hostility and despair. Likewise, instead of regarding the failures he experiences as stepping stones on the road to eventual success, he might regard them simply as traumatic events. John might also be quick to take offense at the things other people say and do, even though they are going out of their way to avoid offending him. His acquaintances might, for these reasons, characterize him (privately) as emotionally brittle. And one more comment is in order: even though John may be a passionate advocate of social justice, it is difficult to imagine him going on to become, say, the next Martin Luther King. Playing such a role would require self-confidence and inner strength, traits that John seems to lack.

One can only imagine how John's great-grandparents, if still alive, would react to his behavior. During World War II, they likely would have experienced many setbacks and might even have had to fight in the war. They nevertheless emerged from the ordeal as functional human beings who, if anything, were stronger and more appreciative of life than they formerly had been. And yet their great-grandson, despite living in peaceful and prosperous times, seems both unhappy and emotionally vulnerable.

Some readers might have had a childhood like John's and, as a result, might now lack resilience. If you are one of them, realize that my goal in comparing you to your great-grandparents is not to make you feel bad but to offer encouragement. If resilience were an innate trait, the way eye color is, you would likely have inherited it from your great-grandparents. The fact that you didn't is therefore evidence that resilience is not an innate trait; it is instead an acquired ability—like the ability to ride a bike or to speak a foreign language. This in turn means that you have it in your power to become more resilient. It will require effort on your part to do so, but the resilience you gain can result in a dramatic improvement in the quality of whatever life you find yourself living. Let us therefore turn our attention, in Part II, to the Stoic advice on how to become more resilient.

PART II

⟨◉◉◉⟩

THE PSYCHOLOGY
OF SETBACKS

CHAPTER 5

You Are of Two Minds

You are a divided being, in the sense of having both a mind and a body. Furthermore, your mind itself is divided into a conscious and a subconscious component. Because of the front-and-center nature of your conscious mind, you are thoroughly familiar with its operations. The same cannot be said, though, of your subconscious mind.

To gain evidence of your subconscious mind's existence, along with insight into its operations, perform the *zazen* meditation. Find a quiet place where you can sit—or better still, lie down—for five minutes. During that time, close your eyes and think of nothing—try, that is, to stop thinking. You will find this exceedingly difficult to do. Ideas will keep popping into your conscious mind, which is to say that your subconscious mind will keep planting them there.

Whereas your conscious mind is conspicuously rational, your subconscious mind operates in a semirational manner. It is capable of coming up with crazy ideas: consider your dreams. It is also susceptible to a variety of unsavory influences. When, for example, you buy something you don't need, it is likely because an advertiser successfully planted an idea in your subconscious mind, which in turn persuaded your conscious mind to make the purchase.

You might think that your conscious mind, thanks to its rational nature, would be in charge, but this is not the case. To the contrary, your conscious mind appears to be perfectly willing to play the role of lackey to your subconscious mind. For example, instead of using its reasoning ability to figure out a way to reduce your burdensome mortgage payments, your conscious mind might spend its time coming up with a clever way to finance the extravagant car that your subconscious mind is convinced you can't live without.

And what is the source of your subconscious mind's power? Stated simply, it doesn't fight fair. If your conscious mind comes up with a sensible reason to dismiss its suggestion, your subconscious mind will simply suggest it again—and again and again. This is why you might find yourself eating a second piece of cake after dinner when, truth be told, you didn't even need the first piece. It is also why, after being talked into having one beer, you might find yourself thirsty for another. The alcohol in the first beer will affect your brain in a way that diminishes your conscious mind's ability to withstand the nagging of your subconscious mind, and as a result, you will find yourself wanting "just one more."

Alternatively, your subconscious mind will sneakily wait until you have gone to bed to present you with an idea. You might put that idea out of your (conscious) mind so you can sleep, only to have it pop back in. As a result, by the time the sun rises, your sleep-deprived conscious mind might have capitulated: it will do whatever your subconscious mind wants, just to shut it up.

WHEN YOU EXPERIENCE A SETBACK, your subconscious mind goes to work trying to fathom its cause, and it is inclined to point an accusing finger: it looks for another person as the cause and likes to attribute sinister motives to that person. More generally, your subconscious mind tends to treat life's setbacks as undeserved tribulations. It therefore tries to convince you that you have been wronged. Shortly thereafter—unless you take steps to prevent it— your emotions will rise in support of your subconscious mind's interpretation of events. But whereas your subconscious mind likes to nag your conscious mind into submission, your emotions shout their demands. As a result, in the aftermath of a setback, you might, much to your surprise, find *yourself* shouting at the person your subconscious mind has accused.

When you experience a setback, your conscious mind can therefore become the target of a double attack—a crossfire, as it were—directed by your subconscious mind and assisted by your emotions. Under these circumstances, your conscious mind will struggle to think clearly, and as a result, you might end up with a second-rate workaround to your setback. And even worse, once your emotions are triggered, they are hard to subdue, so they may continue to disrupt your life long after the setback that triggered them has been overcome. Dealing with your emotions and your subconscious mind, I should add, is a lifelong challenge, since unlike any children you might have, your emotions and subconscious mind are never going to grow up.

YOU MAY RESENT THE ROLE that your emotions and subconscious mind play in your life. They interfere with your ability to cope with the world and thereby make your days more challenging than they need to be. You may also imagine that the ancient Stoics, being eminently rational—they were among the world's first logicians—would have tried to extinguish the operation of the subconscious mind and throttle the emotions. But they did no such thing.

They realized, to begin with, that there is an upside to having a subconscious mind. It can, for example, read body language and facial expressions in a way that is very difficult to put into words. As a result, it can give you a gut feeling that someone is not to be trusted and might thereby prevent you from being exploited. Your subconscious mind also has a moral sense. It turns out that many heroic rescues are triggered not by rational analysis—there simply isn't time for it—but rather by a gut moral instinct about what must be done under certain circumstances.[1] Your subconscious mind is also the source of most of your creative insights. Artists, writers, mathematicians, scientists, and inventors rely heavily on their subconscious mind for break-through ideas.[2] Your subconscious mind is where your muse, if you have one, resides.

That the subconscious mind could provide mathematicians, scientists, and inventors with insights suggests that besides having a wild imagination, it has the ability to reason. And indeed it does, but in a different way than your conscious mind reasons. In particular, your subconscious mind is quite willing to engage in lateral thinking and to explore unlikely connections between ideas, something that your sober and methodical conscious mind is reluctant to do.

The Stoics weren't anti-emotion; indeed, they placed a high value on *positive* emotions, including delight, joy, and a sense of awe. They knew that without these emotions, ours would be a gray existence—and probably pointless as well. At the same time, though, they were intent on reducing the number of *negative* emotions they experienced, including frustration, anger, grief, and disappointment.

This is why they came up with what I am calling the *Stoic test strategy.* To employ it, we assume that the setbacks we experience are not simply undeserved tribulations but tests of our ingenuity and resilience, administered by imaginary Stoic gods. To pass these tests, we must not only come up with effective workarounds to setbacks but must also, while doing so, avoid the onset of negative emotions.

By treating a setback as a Stoic test, we take our subconscious mind out of the setback-response loop. More precisely, we preclude it from suggesting a finger-pointing explanation for a setback, an explanation that assumes that someone else is taking advantage of us or abusing us. This prevents the activation of our emotions, which not only dramatically lowers the personal cost of being set back but also improves our chances of dealing with the setback in a thoughtful manner.

If this were all the Stoic test strategy accomplished, it would be worth our while to employ it in response to a setback. If we are clever in our use of the strategy, though, we can find ourselves not only avoiding negative emotions but also experiencing positive ones, including pride, satisfaction, and maybe even joy, as we rise to meet the challenge the setback represents. The Stoics, in other words, came up with a strategy for turning the setback lemons that life hands us into lemonade—or maybe even a lemon meringue pie.

The discovery and development of the Stoic test strategy is clearly one of the Stoics' greatest accomplishments. In the remainder of this book, I will develop this strategy in greater detail and explore its use. First, however, it will be useful to familiarize ourselves with two psychological phenomena, *anchoring* and *framing*, that lie at the heart of the Stoic test strategy. They were "discovered" in the late twentieth century, two millennia after the Stoics put them to work in their lives and philosophy.

CHAPTER 6

SINKING ANCHORS

In 1974 the psychologists Amos Tversky and Daniel Kahneman did an experiment that made use of a wheel of fortune.[1] It looked like any number between 1 and 100 could come up on their wheel, but in fact it was rigged: only number 10 and number 65 could come up. The wheel was spun one time in the presence of experimental subjects, who were then asked, first, whether the percentage of African nations in the United Nations was higher or lower than the number that came up on the wheel, and second, what they thought the correct percentage was.

Subjects who got 10 as their wheel number guessed, on average, that 25 percent of the nations in the UN were African, whereas those who got 65 as their wheel number guessed 45 percent. This is very strange behavior, since the number that comes up on the wheel obviously has no connection whatsoever with the percentage of African nations in the UN. And yet the wheel number they got had clearly affected their guesses. (In 1974, 36 percent of the nations in the UN were African.)

In a variant of this experiment, the psychologists Fritz Strack and Thomas Mussweiler divided experimental subjects into two groups.[2] Those in the first were asked whether Mahatma Gandhi was over or under 9 years of age when he died and were then asked to guess his age at death. Their average guess was 50. Those in the second group were asked whether Gandhi was over or under 140 years of age when he died and were then asked to guess his age at death. Their average guess was 67, which is 17 years older than the first group guessed. Obviously, Gandhi had to have died after age 9 in order to accomplish all the things he did, and obviously he died before age 140, since no one lives that long. It is therefore surprising that asking the experimental subjects the over-under questions could have such an impact on their guesses about how old he was—and yet it did. (Gandhi in fact died at 78.)

These examples illustrate what has become known as the *anchoring effect*. In Kahneman and Tversky's experiment, the rigged wheel sank an "anchor" into the subconscious minds of their research subjects, and on lodging there, it affected their subsequent speculations about the world. In Strack and Mussweiler's experiment, the over-under question about Gandhi's age played a similar role. In both experiments, a subject's conscious mind lacked sufficient information to make a rational guess, but instead of admitting its ignorance, it yielded the floor to the subject's subconscious mind, which was happy to hazard one. Those guesses, though, were distorted by the anchors that had been sunk into the subject's subconscious mind.

Businesses use anchoring to sell their goods and services. Suppose a clothing store has a shipment of shirts to sell, and the store manager has two retailing options. Plan A is to price the shirts at $32 each. Plan B is to price them at $40 but to have frequent 20-percent-off sales. In either case, consumers will have access to the shirts at $32, but Plan B has the psychological advantage of sinking a $40 "regular-price anchor" into shoppers' subconscious minds. As a result, when the shirts go on sale, customers will have the impression that they are getting a $40 shirt for only $32. This impression will trigger in them a desire to purchase additional shirts, and these added sales, together with a small number of full-price sales[3] at $40 per shirt, means that overall, Plan B will be substantially more profitable than Plan A.

THE ANCIENT STOIC PHILOSOPHERS were way ahead of these psychologists and businessmen. They employed the anchoring phenomenon not to sell shirts but to have a more fulfilling life. In particular, they would periodically make a point of imagining ways in which their lives could be worse. This might sound like a recipe for a miserable existence, but was in fact quite the opposite. By thinking about how things could be worse, they effectively sank an anchor into their subconscious minds (not that they thought in these psychological terms). The presence of that anchor affected how they subsequently felt about their current situation. Instead of comparing it to the superior situations they routinely found themselves dreaming of, they compared it to the inferior situations they imagined and thereupon concluded that things weren't so bad.

This process, now known as *negative visualization*, is one of the most remarkable psychological instruments in the Stoic tool kit. It is important to realize that in advising us to negatively visualize, the Stoics weren't advocating that we *dwell* on how things could be worse; that would indeed be a recipe for misery. Instead, what we should do is periodically have *flickering thoughts* about how our lives and circumstances could be worse.

As an exercise in negative visualization, imagine that you receive a phone call telling you that a close friend has passed away. Give yourself a few seconds for this possibility to sink in. Accompany this thought with a mental image of, say, attending that friend's funeral. This provides the visual component of the negative visualization. Now return to your daily business. There is a very good chance that when you next encounter this friend, you will experience a little burst of delight in her continued existence. This is because you will, if only for a time, have stopped taking that existence for granted.

As another exercise in negative visualization, close your eyes for a few seconds and imagine that you have lost your color vision. Try to imagine a shades-of-gray world. Now open your eyes and inspect your environment. You will likely do so with an altered state of mind. You will start to see—really *see*—the colors that you have been seeing all your life, and you will likely be glad to see them. You will, if only for a time, be grateful that you don't live in the colorless world of a color-blind person.

Those who are color-blind obviously won't be able to do this visualization, but not to worry—here is another exercise. Imagine that you are not just color-blind but blind, period. Imagine that you live in a world of darkness, in which you never see a rose or the face of a loved one. Or instead of simply imagining it, why not live it for a while? As an extension of this exercise, close your eyes and see how long you can keep them closed. When you open them again, you will likely feel a rush of gratitude.

And if you happen to be not just color-blind but completely blind, you can still benefit from negative visualization. You are presumably reading this book in Braille or listening to a recording of it. Imagine, though, that you were instead living in the time before Braille and sound recording existed. Under these circumstances, you would have to find someone willing to read books to you; otherwise, you will be cut off from the world of literature. But you aren't living in that time. Again, aren't you lucky?

Besides thinking about how much worse off you would be if you lost something, you can think about how much worse off you would be if you never had it to begin with. Along these lines, consider the situation of Marcia, a first-century Roman woman who was still profoundly grieving the death of her son after three years. Seneca's advice to her: rather than mourning the end of his life, she should be thankful that her son was able to play a role in her life for as long as he did.[4]

YOU DON'T HAVE TO BE BRILLIANT to practice negative visualization; nor do you need hours of time. To the contrary, you can practice it, for only a few seconds, practically anywhere, and at zero financial cost. That such a basic technique could be so powerful is amazing. Consider it a gift to mankind from the (imaginary) Stoic gods.

It is likewise amazing that such a powerful technique could be so easy to learn. You need not study with a guru on a distant mountaintop, nor practice for years to become proficient. Indeed, by reading the last few paragraphs—seated, I hope, in a comfortable chair—you have learned all you need to know to benefit from the technique. You may even have already benefited from it by doing the exercises I provided.

It is easy to take what we have for granted. Consequently, after a long period in which nothing bad happens, a practicing Stoic might become complacent and forget to do negative visualization. This has happened to me on many occasions. Fortunately for us, the Stoic gods have a way of getting us to think about how things could be worse: they *show* us how they could be worse by presenting us with setbacks. In doing this, they are actually doing us a favor, since a setback, if we deal with it in the proper frame of mind, is likely to trigger in us a renewed appreciation of our life and circumstances.

With a bit of effort and cleverness, you can find a bright lining to almost any cloud you encounter. Almost regardless of how bad things are, they could be worse, and this alone is reason to give thanks.

CHAPTER 7

PLAYING THE FRAME GAME

So much for anchoring. Framing is another curious psychological phenomenon that was employed by the ancient Stoics, only to be rediscovered and studied by modern psychologists. Whereas the use of anchoring can help us better appreciate our lives, the use of framing can prevent setbacks from disrupting our tranquility; indeed, frame events cleverly, and we might even find ourselves welcoming the setbacks we experience! This, I realize, is a pretty remarkable claim to make, so allow me to explain.

I will begin by asking a hypothetical question. Suppose your physician informs you that you have a serious illness and offers you a choice between two medical procedures. One has a one-month survival rate of 90 percent, while the other has a 10 percent mortality rate in the first month. Which would you choose?

Many people will be attracted to the first procedure because of its high survival rate. If you think about it more carefully, though, you will realize that a one-month survival rate of 90 percent is tantamount to a 10 percent mortality rate in the first month. A perfectly rational person would therefore find the two procedures equally attractive. People aren't, however, perfectly rational. In particular, they are influenced by how choices are framed, and a choice framed in terms of survival will seem more attractive than the same choice framed in terms of death. Even highly trained physicians are susceptible to the framing phenomenon.[1]

The Stoic philosophers long ago understood and appreciated the power of framing—not that they used this term to describe it. According to Epictetus, "Another person will not do you harm unless you wish it; you will be harmed at just that time at which you take yourself to be harmed."[2] More generally, he reminds us that "what upsets people is not things themselves but their judgments about the things."[3] Seneca shared this view—"It is not how the wrong is done that matters, but how it is taken"[4]—as did Marcus Aurelius: "If you are distressed by anything external, the pain is not due to the thing itself, but to your estimate of it; and this you have the power to revoke at any moment."[5] The Stoics, in other words, knew that while our subconscious mind is inclined to frame events in ways that trigger negative emotions, we can substantially undermine that tendency by consciously reframing events.

We can, for example, think of our lives as an art gallery, in which the paintings are the events we experience daily. Although we have limited ability to control what paintings hang in this gallery, we have extensive control over how they are framed, and it turns out that framing makes all the difference. A painting that looks hideous in one frame might look sublime in another. In art gallery terms, then, an optimist is someone who customarily places life's paintings into frames that make them look beautiful, and a pessimist is someone who places them into ugly frames.

Stoics, as we have seen, are often caricatured as emotionless, wooden figures, but this simply isn't the case. The Roman Stoics had a reputation for being not just optimistic but positively cheerful. They were vibrantly alive, and many appear to have been admired and even loved by those around them. One of the things that made them attractive was their penchant for seeing the bright side of things—for placing the paintings that life handed them into beautiful frames.

WHEN LIFE PRESENTS US WITH A SETBACK, we have many ways to explain it—many different frames, that is, in which to place it. As we have seen, our subconscious mind tends to assume that it was other people who set us back and that they did so on purpose and even with malice. I will refer to this as the *blame frame*. Once our subconscious mind has done this, our emotions will be aroused, and we will likely get angry. What could have been merely a setback transmogrifies into an ordeal.

Fortunately, our conscious mind has the ability to undermine the operation of our subconscious mind. In particular, by coming up with alternative explanations for our setbacks, it puts them in frames that are neutral or even beautiful. It thereby prevents negative emotions from being triggered, and it can even give rise to positive emotions. Let us, therefore, explore some of the alternative frames that are available to the conscious mind.

The competing obligations frame: Suppose someone refuses to give you something you hope to get. Your subconscious mind will likely provide a blame frame for this setback: the person in question is cheating you. As a result, you might find yourself getting angry. There are, however, other ways to explain your failure to get what you expected. The person deciding what you got may be enmeshed in a web of obligations, meaning that if she gives you what you want, she will be unable to give others what they deserve. If this is indeed the case, it would be wrong for you to get what you expected, and it would therefore be unreasonable for you to get angry for not getting it. By framing this setback as a consequence of competing obligations, you can avoid experiencing a number of negative emotions.

The incompetence frame: Suppose a hotel clerk loses your reservation. Yes, he may have done so on purpose, but more likely he is simply incompetent. Frame the incident as incompetence rather than malice, and the emotion you subsequently experience might be pity rather than anger.

The storytelling frame: When you have been set back, think in terms of the setback story you might tell in the future. It may be a story about how frustrated you were, how mean and stupid people are, and how unfair the world is. It can, in other words, be a truly boring story, the essence of which people have likely heard hundreds of times before. With a little effort on your part, though, you can "write," with your behavior, a story that is not just interesting but potentially uplifting to those who hear it.

Thinking in terms of future storytelling can take much of the sting out of the setbacks you experience. This is because your attention will be focused not on how you are being wronged but on what you must do to bring the story to a satisfying conclusion. And if events take a strange turn in the aftermath of a setback, you may, rather than getting even more upset, feel grateful. It puts, after all, an interesting wrinkle into your setback story.

At this point, a clarification is in order. Using the storytelling frame does *not* mean that after muddling angrily through a setback, you *make up* a story about how wonderfully you handled it. The story you tell *must be true.* So for you to *come off as* resilient and competent in your story, you must *actually be* resilient and competent in your handling of the setback.

Realize, too, that if a Roman Stoic like Epictetus employed the storytelling frame, he might not subsequently share the story he had "written" with other people. His primary goal in employing this frame, after all, would have been to avoid experiencing negative emotions in the aftermath of a setback, something he already would have accomplished by the time storytelling opportunities arose. Furthermore, if he *did* subsequently share the story, it would likely be for one of two reasons. The first would be to make people aware of a workaround for a setback they had experienced or might experience. The second would be to show a pessimistic person that experiencing a setback needn't trigger negative emotions; indeed, it can even trigger positive emotions. How about that!

Something Epictetus would *not* have done is share his setback stories with others in an attempt to impress them with his resilience and ingenuity. He knew full well that the values by which he and the other Roman Stoics lived were uncommon. Whereas most people valued fame and fortune,[6] a Stoic's primary goal in life was to attain and then maintain tranquility—to avoid, that is, experiencing negative emotions while continuing to enjoy positive emotions. He also knew that when people judge others, they do so in accordance with their own values, not in accordance with the values of the people they are judging. He therefore concluded that a sensible Stoic will ignore the praise of non-Stoics, so it would be pointless for him to go out of his way to gain that praise by sharing his setback stories.

Epictetus even went so far as to suggest that we should take non-Stoics' praise as a kind of reverse indicator of our progress as Stoics: "If people think you amount to something," he said, "distrust yourself."[7] He might likewise take other people's criticism of him as evidence that, as a practicing Stoic, he was on the right track. This sounds perverse, I know, but look at the unhappy people around you. The surest way to win their praise is to adopt and live in accordance with their values. It will then be easy for them to praise you, because by doing so, they are indirectly praising themselves. The snag, of course, is that by sharing their values you will likely end up sharing their misery.

The comedic frame: When someone wrongs you, keep in mind Seneca's comment that "laughter, and a lot of it, is the right response to the things which drive us to tears!"[8] He also reminded us that this technique was employed by Socrates. After someone boxed his ears, Socrates responded not by getting angry but by commenting on how unfortunate it is, when we set out for a walk, that we can't know ahead of time whether to wear a helmet.[9]

I came across a wonderful example of the use of humor in the face of a setback while touring Machu Picchu in Peru. My guide said that a few years earlier, he had been leading a group of Australians on a four-day hike along the Inca Trail in the Andes Mountains. When the hike ended, the group returned to Aguas Calientes, a nearby town, where they would catch the train to Cusco, in order to board their flight back home. But then my guide found out the train wouldn't be running for days—the Urubamba River was in flood stage, meaning that his clients were stuck in Aguas Calientes. When he informed them, they fell silent, until one of the Australians offered a brilliant response: "Well, then, let's have some beer!" The rest of the group laughed, and off they went to a nearby bar.

By responding to the setback with humor, the Australian not only prevented anger from arising in himself but set the tone for the group. His joke effectively cut off the sort of complaining that might otherwise have filled the vacuum. Once he played the beer card, it would have been very difficult for someone else to say, "I've got a better idea: let's stand around and moan about how unfair life is." Notice, too, that by going for beer, the Australians transformed a setback into a great story to share with friends in the future—a story about the time they got stuck in Aguas Calientes.

Another time humor comes in handy is when we have been insulted.[10] Lots of people respond to insults by getting angry, and the insult thereby sets them back. A better response is simply to laugh. By doing so, we not only forestall anger in ourselves but make the person who insulted us look like a fool: he hit us with his best verbal shot, and we just laughed it off.

Laughter can also be an effective response to a profound personal calamity. Roger Ebert realized this. So did Michael Cubiss, a lively and fit former military officer who started an import business. At age forty, a massive cerebral hemorrhage left him "locked in," not to the extent that Jean-Dominique Bauby was, but severely enough to limit his ability to engage in everyday activities. Cubiss responded to his predicament not by lapsing into depression but by using his well-developed sense of humor to make jokes about his ludicrous circumstances.[11] Conclusion: if you can bring yourself to laugh at the things that make most people cry, you have a powerful weapon to use against life's adversities.

As we have seen, Socrates made a joke in response to a physical attack. Some might criticize this response on moral grounds: rather than simply laughing at his attacker, shouldn't Socrates have turned him in to the police?[12] Doing this, after all, would decrease the chance that the attacker would attack Socrates or some other innocent person in the future.

In response to this criticism, let me point out that using the comedic frame does not preclude us from turning in an attacker. By framing the attack, we can prevent it from harming us emotionally, and this is important to do, since the emotional harm we experience in the aftermath of an attack can far outweigh the physical harm. After that, we have the option of taking steps to prevent similar attacks on ourself and others in the future. Depending on the circumstances, this might mean turning in the attacker to the authorities. I should add that the historical record does not indicate whether this is what Socrates did.

The game frame: Consider the following scenario: while you are running, someone comes up from behind and tackles you to the ground. How would you react? Given only this much information, you might instinctively place the event in a blame frame: you have been wronged and will be quite angry at the brute responsible for the attack.

But before we go any further, let me add one more element to the above scenario: at the time you were tackled from behind, you were playing rugby, and the tackle was legal under rugby rules. Under such circumstances, it would be absurd for you to point an accusing finger and place the event in a blame frame. You should instead place it in what might be called a *game frame*. Getting tackled is, after all, part of the game of rugby, and if you didn't want to get tackled, you should have stayed off the field of play.

Although getting tackled might count as a setback in the context of a rugby game, it is a setback you must shrug off if you are to play rugby effectively. Furthermore, rather than treating the tackler like a criminal, you should treat him, as long as he didn't break any rules, as a worthy competitor on the field of play. By employing the game frame, we can take much of the sting out of events that would otherwise be traumatic. It is therefore surprising that we don't employ this frame more often.

The author Jean Liedloff tells a story that nicely illustrates the power of game framing. As a young woman, she was invited by two Italian men to go diamond hunting in Venezuela. It sounded like a wonderful adventure, so she accepted the invitation. They hired several South American Indians as laborers and obtained a heavy and cumbersome dugout canoe in which to travel.

At one point in the journey, they had to carry the canoe over jagged rocks in the tropical sun, with Liedloff doing her share of the carrying. All of them got cut, bruised, and seared by the sun-heated rocks. In the course of the portage, though, she noticed that whereas the Italians were treating each cut and bump as another setback and cursing in response, the Indians were treating the experience as a game. The canoe's unpredictable movements made them laugh. Getting pinned against hot rocks by the canoe was for them not grounds for complaint but an excuse for more laughter. Her account of the episode:

> All were doing the same work; all were experiencing strain and pain. There was no difference in our situa-

tions except that we had been conditioned by our culture to believe that such a combination of circumstances constituted an unquestionable low on the scale of wellbeing and were quite unaware that we had any option in the matter. The Indians, on the other hand, equally unconscious of making a choice, were in a particularly merry state of mind, reveling in the camaraderie; and, of course, they had had no long build-up of dread to mar the preceding days. Each forward move was for them a little victory.[13]

She decided to join the Indians in framing the endeavor as a game and found that it made the rest of the trip much easier. By framing a setback as a component of a game, we can dramatically reduce its emotional impact. And the game in question needn't be a formal game like rugby; it can be an impromptu game, like the Indians' canoe game.

The Stoic test frame: The last frame that we shall consider has gamelike elements: when confronted by a setback, the Stoics say, we should pretend that imaginary Stoic gods are testing us with our well-being in mind. To pass this test—and thereby win the game—we must stay calm while finding a workaround for the setback. It is a fanciful frame, to be sure, but a useful one nonetheless.

The ancient Stoics knew that although we have limited control over what setbacks we experience, we have considerable discretion in how we frame them and hence considerable control over how they affect us. People normally think of setbacks as annoying events, or even worse, as undeserved tribulations; as a result, they respond by getting frustrated or angry. By choosing another frame, we can keep our cool in the face of a setback and thereby increase our chances of finding the optimal workaround. And not only that, but by employing the Stoic test frame, we can interpret setbacks as interesting challenges, thereby deriving a degree of satisfaction from dealing with them. This sounds amazing, I know, but it's true, so let us take a closer look at the Stoic test strategy.

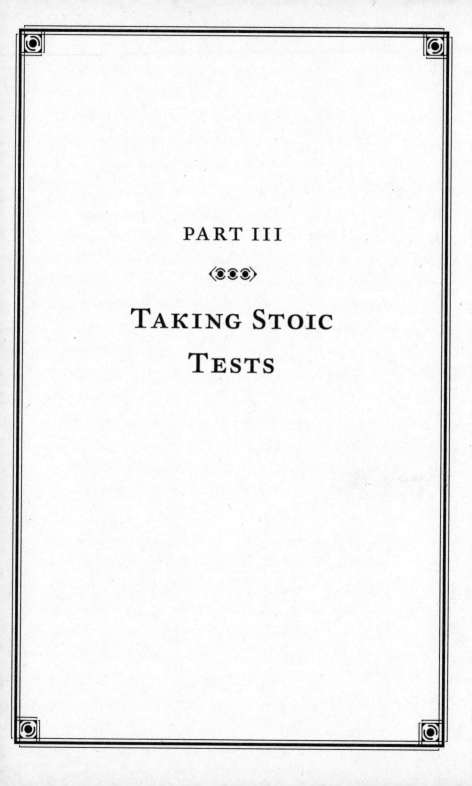

PART III

TAKING STOIC
TESTS

CHAPTER 8

Your *Other* Setback
Challenge

Besides the obvious challenge of finding a workaround for a setback, we face a second challenge: *preventing ourselves from experiencing negative emotions in the aftermath of that setback*. Many people overlook this second challenge, for the simple reason that they don't think it is in their power to control their post-setback emotions. Yes, they get upset, angry, or depressed, but that's just what people do, right?

This attitude is unfortunate for a number of reasons. Getting angry in response to a setback will shatter whatever tranquility we were formerly experiencing. It will also cloud our thinking, making it difficult for our conscious mind to develop possible workarounds. As a result, we will probably end up choosing one that is less than optimal.

Consider two people stuck in adjacent cars in a traffic jam. One responds by getting angry. He curses the other drivers. He calls his wife and tells her how angry he is, quite possibly causing her a degree of distress as well. When he finally gets to work, he is gruff with his co-workers, who might respond by returning the bad attitude.

Another driver, by contrast, quickly realizes that there is nothing he can do to make the traffic move faster. He therefore turns his attention away from the jam and toward the opportunity the delay affords him. As his car sits immobile, he checks his e-mail. He notices a new episode of his favorite podcast, so he starts listening to it. When he arrives at his destination, he is late, but he is in a good mood. If someone asks how the traffic was, he might answer, truthfully and without drama, that it was pretty slow. For this driver, the traffic jam will be nothing more than a small wrinkle in the fabric of his day.

Suppose you are facing the challenge of a burst water pipe in your house or apartment. As a result of the break, you might not have water for your morning shower or coffee. The broken pipe itself, however, is relatively easy to fix. It might take a plumber only twenty minutes to do so, and it might take an accomplished do-it-yourselfer a few hours, including the trip to the hardware store.

But when a water pipe bursts, the ruptured pipe is only one of the problems that confront you. Besides the problem of not having water where you *do* want it, you have the much bigger problem of having a lot of water where you *don't* want it. This unwanted water might flood several rooms, and if the broken pipe is on an upper story, it might cause the lower-story ceiling to collapse. The flooding problem is much more serious than that of the break in the pipe itself. Consequently, when a water pipe bursts, your first response should not be to try to mend the pipe, or to go out and buy drinking water so you can make your morning coffee. It should be to turn off the water supply, to prevent your dwelling from getting flooded.

In parallel manner, when you experience a setback, you are faced with not one challenge but two, and the second—*preventing a flood of negative emotions*—is usually more critical than the first. This emotional challenge may be secondary in terms of time and causation, but it is often the primary challenge in terms of its impact on us. Usually the harm done us by our emotions—if we allow them to be triggered—is the biggest cost associated with a setback. A sensible person will realize this, and on experiencing a setback, her first response will be to take the steps necessary to prevent the onset of negative emotions. Notice that I didn't say she will find a way to *conceal* those emotions; she will *prevent them from arising*, so there won't be any negative emotions to conceal.

MANY READERS WILL ADMIT THAT it is stupid to get angry about being stuck in a traffic jam. This anger simply upsets us without having any impact on our situation. Aren't there cases, though, in which the expression of anger is not just permissible but advisable?

Somewhat surprisingly, Seneca agrees that such cases exist. Suppose you are dealing with someone who has a "sluggish mind" and who therefore doesn't respond to requests—even those that are perfectly reasonable—unless they are accompanied by a display of anger. It would be understandable, Seneca says, for you to respond to this person's forwardness with anger, but he has a better idea: respond with *feigned* anger.[1] Doing this will likely achieve the results you are hoping for without making you pay the emotional price of actually getting angry.

Another case in which it might be argued that we should let ourselves experience anger is one in which a grave injustice has been done. In such cases, the anger we experience will be righteous indignation, a very special kind of anger. Indeed, failure to experience righteous indignation might, under some circumstances, be taken as evidence of a flaw in our moral character.

This is an interesting theory, but when we look back in history, we find that it is quite possible to passionately devote ourselves to fighting injustice without our hearts being filled with anger. Consider, for example, Mahatma Gandhi, who fought the unjust treatment of Indians by their British rulers, as well as the unjust treatment of "untouchables" by higher-caste Indians, in a determinedly peaceable manner. Consider also Gandhi admirer Martin Luther King, who fought the injustice of racism. Although King sometimes gave passionate speeches, he does not appear to have been an angry man. Yes, he was capable of experiencing flashes of anger, as any person is, but he apparently did his best to quell them.

In his *Autobiography*, King told the story of his role in the

1955 bus boycott in Montgomery, Alabama. The boycott in question was triggered by the arrest of Rosa Parks for refusing to give up her seat to a white man. The whites-only section of the bus was full, and bus rules allowed the driver to expand this section so that subsequently boarding whites would have a seat, even if this deprived blacks of theirs. Furthermore, the whites-only section would be expanded not a seat at a time but a row at a time, in part to spare whites the indignity of having to sit in the same row as a black. Parks and three other blacks were occupying the row of seats just behind the whites-only section, so they were all told to move farther back into the colored section. The other three blacks acceded to the demand, but Parks refused, so the driver had her arrested.

The black community was outraged and decided to boycott Montgomery's buses. King was chosen as their primary negotiator. In this role, he had to deal with both white racists and outraged blacks. He soon found himself getting angry at people on both sides but quickly regretted doing so: "I knew that this was no way to solve a problem. 'You must not harbor anger,' I admonished myself. 'You must be willing to suffer the anger of the opponent, and yet not return anger. You must not become bitter. No matter how emotional your opponents are, you must be calm.'"[2]

Many of those involved in today's social change movements equate anger with passion: if you truly care about an injustice, you will be angry about it. They may go on to explain that anger is an effective tool in fights for justice, as it motivates us, and publicly expressed righteous anger gets the attention of the people we are trying to persuade.

This may be true, but as the Stoics well knew, anger is a double-edged sword: besides motivating us, it can exhaust us, so that we run out of energy before winning our battle. Furthermore, the anger we express often triggers anger in those on the other side of an issue. They harden their stance, making compromise less likely. We live in a world in which change, when it comes, is likely to be incremental, meaning that righteous anger can retard progress on the issue in question. And finally, we know that anger can cloud our judgment, causing us to do foolish things and blinding us to possible solutions.

Many social reformers feel so strongly about an issue that they are willing to make personal sacrifices to accomplish their goals. By allowing themselves to get angry, they are clearly sacrificing; anger, as I've said, is incompatible with joy. What is less clear is that making these sacrifices will help them achieve their goals; indeed, it might be counterproductive. Social reformers are therefore wise to follow in the footsteps of Gandhi and King, and stay calm while working passionately to bring about change.

SO MUCH FOR ANGER in response to setbacks. What about grief? If someone close to you dies, grief is the natural response. Furthermore, according to Elisabeth Kübler-Ross, grief is the psychologically appropriate response to a personal loss. If we suppress our grief, she says, we increase our chances of experiencing serious mental distress in the future.

Kübler-Ross's theory of grief has been challenged. The psychologist Robert J. Kastenbaum, for one, has argued that the theory is not sufficiently supported by empirical data.[3] Furthermore, even if Kübler-Ross had demonstrated the existence of five stages of grief, it would leave open the question of whether making an effort to go through them is the best way to deal with grief.

George Bonanno, a professor of clinical psychology at Columbia University, argues that we are much more resilient than Kübler-Ross would have us believe and are therefore much less in need of grief counseling than many psychologists recommend—and make a living providing. Indeed, his research indicates that most people, left to themselves, will rebound from an interpersonal loss, and that grief counseling can make things worse by inadvertently undermining their resilience.[4]

Consider the death of a loved one. Seneca acknowledged that some grief is appropriate in its aftermath—"Nature requires from us some sorrow"—but adds that "more than this is the result of vanity."[5] He has in mind those individuals whose primary motivation for public displays of grief is to show the world how sensitive and caring they are. The Stoics were also aware that in some cases, the anguish a person experiences after a death is motivated more by feelings of guilt than by grief. Suppose a husband takes his wife for granted while she is alive and consequently does not invest as much into their relationship as he should. After she is gone, he can no longer make things right, and this thought sickens him.

The people we love won't be with us forever—if nothing else, our own death will deprive us of their company. The Stoics therefore recommend that we periodically make a point of reminding ourselves just how wonderful it is that the people we love are currently part of our life. Something could have happened that deprived us of their company, but it didn't. Aren't we lucky?

Engage in this kind of "mortality meditation," say Stoics, and we will fully appreciate the existence of those we love while they are still alive, meaning that our love can make a difference in their lives. We will therefore feel less need, when they are no longer with us, to grieve their passing. In particular, we won't have regrets about what we could and should have done while they were alive, since we likely would have done it. It should be clear that rather than being ghoulish, these meditations are a deeply life-affirming exercise.

If we presented a Stoic with the list of Kübler-Ross's five stages of grief, his response would be to skip the first four—denial, anger, bargaining, and depression—and go directly to stage five, acceptance. The Stoic would add that since we don't have it in our power to resurrect the dead, we are wasting our time mourning their passing excessively. To the extent possible, we should simply accept their death and get on with life.

CHAPTER 9

USING THE STOIC
TEST STRATEGY

As we have seen, our interpretation of an event is like the frame of a painting. Put a Rembrandt in one sort of frame, and it will look hideous; switch it to another, and it will look sublime. The same is true of the setbacks we experience. Put a setback in one psychological frame, and we will find it upsetting; put it in another, and we may discover, much to our amazement, that we enjoy dealing with that setback.

As we have also seen, when you encounter a setback, your subconscious mind goes into action. It tries to make sense of what is going on by providing a frame for the setback. But even though it has lots of frames to choose from, it tends to favor the *blame frame*: it assumes that you have been wronged, that some person or group of people has it in for you. This likely triggers anger in you, which in turn makes it harder for you to deal with the setback.

Stoics recommend that when we experience a setback, we make a point of consciously framing it as a kind of test. Allow ourselves to get frustrated, and we get a low grade; allow ourselves to become angry or despondent—or even worse, regard ourselves as victims—and we fail. Ideally, the setback won't give rise to negative emotions within us, not because we are successfully concealing our distress but because we have no distress to conceal.

LET US EXPLORE THE STOIC TEST STRATEGY in greater detail. The idea that we treat a setback as a test gives rise to an obvious question: who or what is administering the test? Seneca suggested that "God" is behind it. Before unpacking this suggestion, though, I should explain that the Roman concept of God was rather different from that of modern Christians. For one thing, the Romans didn't have one God; they had several, and their head god, Jupiter, was very much unlike the God of Christianity. Case in point: Jupiter, a married god at the time, assumed the form of a bull so he could seduce—or was it rape?—the goddess Europa, something that the God of Christianity would never dream of doing.

According to Seneca, God (think Jupiter) sets us back not to punish us but to give us an opportunity to do something courageous and thereby increase our chances of attaining "the highest possible excellence." God, Seneca explains, hardens, reviews, and disciplines those who have won his approval and love; but those whom he seems to favor, whom he seems to spare, he is keeping soft against the misfortunes that are to come. You are wrong if you think anyone has been exempted from ill; the man who has known happiness for many a year will receive his share some day; whoever seems to have been set free from this has only been granted a delay.[1]

We should therefore be flattered if we encounter setbacks. Paradoxically, it is evidence that we have caught the attention of God—indeed, that he regards us as a candidate for achieving human excellence. God, says Seneca, knows that "a man needs to be put to the test if he is to gain self-knowledge" and that "only by trying does he learn what his capacities are."[2]

Seneca provides several analogies[3] to help us appreciate God's motives in setting us back. God, he says, resembles a Roman head of household who "does not pamper a good man like a favorite slave; he puts him to the test, hardens him, and makes him ready for his service." Seneca's God resembles a strict father who "orders his children to be roused early to pursue their studies, not allowing them to be idle even on a holiday, and wrings from them sweat and sometimes tears." This fatherly God wants his children to "know the pain of toil, of suffering, of loss, so that they may acquire true strength." He resembles an army general who sends a soldier to carry out a dangerous mission. That soldier won't, if he is brave, think that the general has done him a bad turn. He will instead conclude that the general thinks him brave and daring enough to accomplish the mission. It is, if anything, a sign of favor. God also resembles a teacher who requires "greater effort from the ones who inspire the surer hope."

Epictetus agrees with Seneca regarding God's goals. At one point in his *Discourses*, he imagines a conversation in which God explains why humans experience setbacks:

> If it had been possible, Epictetus, I [God] would have ensured that your poor body and petty possessions were free and immune from hindrance. But as things are, you mustn't forget that this body isn't truly your own, but is nothing more than cleverly moulded clay. But since I couldn't give you that, I've given you a certain portion of myself, this faculty of motivation to act and not to act, of desire and aversion, and, in a word, the power to make proper use of impressions; if you pay good heed to this, and entrust all that you have to its keeping, you'll never be hindered, never obstructed, and you'll never groan, never find fault, and never flatter anyone at all.[4]

We humans, in other words, are hybrid creatures, part god and part animal. Our conscious mind, with its reasoning ability, is our godly component; our subconscious mind and emotions together form our animal component. Epictetus tells us that "it is difficulties that reveal what men amount to; and so, whenever you're struck by a difficulty, remember that God, like a trainer in the gymnasium, has matched you against a tough young opponent." And why would God do such a thing? "So that you may become an Olympic victor; and that is something that can't be achieved without sweat."[5]

Seneca, by the way, also makes reference to athletes in explaining the rationale for Stoic tests: "We see wrestlers . . . matching themselves with only the strongest opponents, and requiring those who prepare them for a bout to use all their strength against them; they expose themselves to blows and hurt, and if they do not find one man to match them, they take on several at a time."[6] They know that "excellence withers without an adversary."[7]

AT THIS POINT, you might be getting nervous: you don't believe in the existence of Jupiter, so how can you use the Stoic test frame? If you believe in the existence of the God of Christianity, you have an easy solution: you can assume that he is testing you to make you stronger, to develop your character, and to make you more appreciative of the life you are living. These are things we would expect a loving father to do, and the God of Christianity, we are told, is the ultimate loving father. Something similar can be done if you are a Muslim who believes in the existence of Allah.

Suppose, however, that like me, you don't believe in the existence of Jupiter, the God of Christianity, or Allah. You can still employ the Stoic test strategy by believing your test givers to be imaginary Stoic gods. Although you know full well they don't exist, they can still play a significant psychological role in your life. By invoking these beings, you are playing the frame game described in Chapter 7: you are framing the setbacks you experience in a manner that will profoundly alter your emotional response to them. For most people, setbacks are merely unfortunate events; with the judicious use of framing, you can turn the setbacks you experience into vehicles for self-transformation.

For me, the Stoic gods are a convenient fiction. If you are a parent, you have likely had experience with such fictions. When your children were young and Christmas was coming, you might have invoked Santa Claus to get them to behave: "If you're mean to the cat, Santa isn't going to bring you very many presents." It is a stimulus to which children respond. By employing the Stoic test strategy, your conscious mind can likewise shape the behavior of your credulous and rather childlike subconscious mind. It sounds strange, I know, but it works.

Those who feel uncomfortable thinking in terms of even imaginary gods can take themselves to be tested by, say, an imaginary father, general, teacher, or coach. Indeed, on occasion, I take myself to be tested not by Stoic gods but by the ghost of Seneca. And in a deeper sense, the ghost of Seneca *does* exist. Because I have read his works, Seneca haunts my intellect, occasionally offering me a compliment but much more often raising his ghostly eyebrows at me in a look of dismay. Regardless of the imaginary tester we choose, the key thing is that we assume that we are being tested for our own good.

As a result of my encounters with the (imaginary) Stoic gods,

I have gained insight into their nature. They are, to begin with, quite powerful. They can cause me to cut myself while shaving and to trip on a root while walking through the woods. When I am at the airport, they can delay or even cancel the flight I am scheduled to take. Indeed, a disproportionate number of the setbacks I experience take place at airports, which has led me to wonder whether this is where the Stoic gods reside.

The Stoic gods can also cause traffic jams and give people the flu. They have it in their power to bring on inconvenient thunderstorms and devastating earthquakes. They are also remarkably tech savvy. Recently, I was looking for airplane tickets online and came across the ideal tickets at a bargain price. In the minute or two that it took me to enter my information to procure them, the Stoic gods fiddled with the Internet in such a manner that the price rose by $100 per ticket. Perhaps someday, just to keep me off balance, they could surprise me with a similarly sized price drop?

The Stoic gods, I have found, possess a mischievous sense of humor. Instead of causing my cell phone to stop working, as they could easily do, they might cause me to accidentally drop it into a glass of lemonade, producing the same result. Such things do happen.

On occasion, instead of causing me to experience a setback, the Stoic gods are content to send me a reminder of the setbacks they can cause. Recently, for example, I was driving to a friend's home. I had been there only a few times before, so I asked my cell phone for directions. It quickly provided them, along with a prediction that the trip would take one hour and four minutes. I knew this couldn't be right, since my friend's house is only a few miles away, so I examined the screen more closely. It turned out that my cell phone, instead of giving me *driving* directions, had given me *walking* directions—additional evidence of the technological savvy of the Stoic gods.

Isn't it wonderful, I thought, *that I can get where I'm going in the comfort of my car rather than having to walk for more than an hour through a cold winter night?* I thanked the Stoic gods for this possible-setback reminder and drove off into the night. And as I drove, I reflected on how remarkable it is that I possess a handheld device that, in response to a verbal request, is capable of giving me audible directions for how to get practically anywhere I want to go, either on foot or by car.

THE GODS WHO ADMINISTER STOIC TESTS do not grade them. You must therefore grade them yourself, and in coming up with a grade, you should take two things into account. The first is how you conducted your search for a workaround for the setback. Before committing to a course of action, did you consider your options? In doing so, did you engage in lateral thinking—did you think "outside the box"? And was the workaround that you finally chose optimal?

An optimal workaround, by the way, won't necessarily be a pleasant workaround. To be optimal, it need only be less unpleasant than the other possible workarounds. Along these lines, getting a foot amputated won't be pleasant, but if the foot is severely gangrenous, amputation will be preferable to the next-best option—death.

The second but more significant factor in grading your performance will be your emotional response to the setback. If you remain calm and collected, you will be worthy of, say, a B. If your goal is to get an A or even an A+ on the exam, though, you will have to do more than remain calm; you will have to welcome the setback and even perk up a bit on its appearance. In this respect, you need to resemble a fireman who, after years of training, is finally called on to put out a fire. At last, a chance to show his stuff!

Notice that the two components of a Stoic test can receive different grades. You can hit on the optimal workaround to a setback but get quite upset over being set back, in which case your workaround grade will be high but your more important emotional-response grade will be low. Or you can stay calm while coming up with a less-than-optimal workaround, in which case your workaround grade will be low but your emotional-response grade will be high. It will often be the case, though, that the lower your emotional-response grade is, the lower your workaround grade will be: it is, after all, hard to think clearly and find the optimal workaround if you are angry, grieving, or despondent.

Before turning the page, take a few minutes to consider the

setbacks you have recently experienced—or, if you have started keeping the journal described in Chapter 1, take a look at the setbacks you've recorded there. How would you grade your responses to them? Are you satisfied with this grade? And if not, what can you do to improve your grade on future setbacks?

CHAPTER 10

THE FIVE-SECOND RULE

As we have seen, when a water pipe bursts, our first priority should be to turn off the water. Only then should we start thinking about cleaning up the mess the water has made, getting the pipe fixed, and getting water for coffee. And the sooner we turn off the water, the better.

In like fashion, when we experience a setback—including those that don't involve a burst pipe—our first priority should be to prevent ourselves from being flooded by negative emotions. Experiencing such emotions would, after all, make it that much harder for us to find and implement the optimal workaround for the setback. Also, these emotions, once they erupt, can do us more harm than the setback itself does.

The key to successfully implementing the Stoic test strategy is to act fast. In the Introduction, I described my response to a canceled airline flight: as soon as I realized that I would not be sleeping in my own bed that night, I invoked the Stoic test strategy. Had I been slow to do so, my subconscious mind would likely have framed it as an undeserved tribulation, negative emotions would have been triggered, and I probably would have spent that night and part of the next day in an angry, frustrated state of mind. By quickly framing the episode as a test, I could focus my thoughts and energy on finding and implementing the best workaround for the setback. Even more important, I was able to retain my equanimity despite being set back.

Most people are familiar with the conventional "five-second rule." It says that if food falls on the floor, we can safely eat it as long as we pick it up within five seconds of when it hit the ground. (The reliability of this rule has not, by the way, been established by any recognized medical authority.) Those employing the Stoic test strategy can think in terms of a similar rule: if we are set back, we have five seconds to declare the event to be a Stoic test.

Even though I have been using the Stoic test strategy for years, there are still occasions when, after being set back, I respond by blurting out a profanity—or should I say, something that back in the twentieth century would have counted as one. These outbursts seem to be reflexive, the way it's reflexive for my knee to jerk when the doctor taps it with that little hammer. Fortunately, such blurting does not seem to prevent me from subsequently being able to employ the Stoic test strategy with success, as long as I do so without delay. And for the record, I have found that the more Stoic tests I take, the less common my setback-related verbal outbursts have become. A sign, perhaps, of Stoic progress?

Besides writing the Declaration of Independence, Thomas Jefferson wrote a document that has since become known as "Ten Rules for a Good Life." One rule is that when someone does something that makes us angry, we should count to ten before we speak—and count to one hundred if we are very angry. The idea is that by counting to ten, our anger will have sufficiently subsided that when we do speak, we won't blurt out something that we will later regret. Notice, by the way, that it takes about five seconds to count to ten.

There is, however, an important difference between Jefferson's count-to-ten rule and my Stoic test version of the five-second rule. Jefferson's rule tells us what to do when we get angry. He is therefore offering damage-control advice. The five-second rule, by contrast, is designed to prevent anger from arising in the first place. In other words, whereas Jefferson was interested in anger management, the Stoics were interested in anger prevention.

IF WE WERE TO GO BACK 500 million years in our extended family tree,[1] we would find ancestors with very simple brains that could do little more than control various bodily functions, sense the outside world, and respond reflexively to that sensory input. Move forward 250 million years from that, and we would find animals that had acquired a limbic system that caused some physical experiences (such as eating food or having sex) to feel good and other experiences (such as getting cut or burned) to feel bad.

Being incentivized in this manner allowed these animals to move beyond purely reflexive behavior. They could go out of their way to do things that felt good and avoid doing things that felt bad.

Have you ever wondered why orgasms are possible? It is because animals capable of experiencing them were more likely to mate and thereby have offspring than animals that weren't. Likewise, have you ever wondered why we feel unpleasantly hungry if we go without eating for a long period and why we feel good when we do eat? It is because animals capable of having these feelings were more likely to stay nourished and therefore to survive than those that lacked them. An animal that thought fasting felt great and sex felt awful would have been unlikely to have any descendants. According to evolutionary biologists, this is how we came to possess the wiring that allows us to feel physically good and bad.[2]

With the passage of many generations, animals' ability to feel good and bad gained another dimension: besides being able to experience physical feelings, they started experiencing mental feelings—also known as emotions. At first, these emotions were probably negative. Animals might, in particular, have come to fear things that experience told them would feel physically bad: after being bitten by a snake, they might develop a fear of snakes.

With the passage of many more generations, these emotions became more complex. If, for example, animals returned to the place where they had been bitten by a snake, they might experience anxiety, another negative emotion, even though no snake was visible. And besides experiencing negative emotions, they would have started experiencing positive emotions. Suppose, for example, that one of our human ancestors threw a spear at a game animal. If it missed its target, the hunter might have experienced disappointment, a negative emotion, but if the spear found its target, he might have experienced a pleasant feeling of accomplishment.

When their brains developed even further, our ancestors were rewarded for forming and subsequently achieving long-term goals. Each significant step they completed on their way to a goal was rewarded with a feeling of accomplishment, and on achieving their ultimate goal, they were rewarded with one of life's greatest pleasures, the rush of success. These good feelings were made possible by a release of the neurotransmitter dopamine in their brain.

Suppose that because you are lazy or lack self-confidence, you refuse to undertake difficult challenges. You thereby deprive yourself of the chance to experience the rush of success—unless, that is, you have access to cocaine. A hit of this drug will cause your brain to release copious amounts of dopamine, and as a result, you will experience a high very similar to the one you would experience on, say, sinking the game-winning shot in the championship basketball game. It is, to be sure, a risky and potentially addictive way to obtain this feeling.

Because our ancestors were social animals, their well-being depended on their position within the social hierarchy. This in turn gave rise to social emotions. If someone snubbed them, they might feel humiliated, and if the incident jeopardized their social standing, they might get mad. They also started experiencing envy toward those above them in the hierarchy. These and other social emotions prompted them to behave in a manner likely to improve their social standing and thereby increase their chances of surviving and reproducing.

We inherited our brain and its emotion-generating wiring from these ancestors. The thing to realize is that although we have added processing power to that brain, its basic wiring hasn't changed much, and as a result, we experience many of the same emotions as they did. Our environment is, however, radically different from theirs. One of their big challenges was getting enough food to eat; one of ours is to avoid getting heart disease as a result of overindulging in cheap and readily available food. They had to worry about getting attacked by animals; we might worry about paying our bills or losing our job. Our brain, then, might be described as a computer with lots of processing power but an archaic operating system. It is our lot in life to be stuck with such a computer.

The ancient Stoics hit on a way to hack that computer. They recognized the human tendency to blame setbacks on someone else and then to get angry at that person. They also realized that if we acted quickly, we could short-circuit this process. In particular, by framing the setback as a test of our resilience and ingenuity, we could not only prevent the onset of negative emotions but transform the setback into a challenge that we might enjoy undertaking. What for most people would simply have been an unpleasant incident might, for us, turn out to be kind of fun.

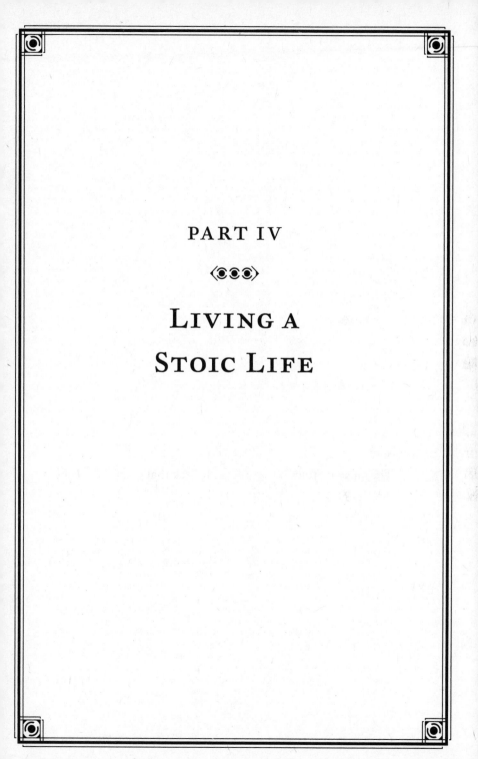

PART IV

⟨●●●⟩

LIVING A
STOIC LIFE

CHAPTER 11

STUDYING FOR STOIC TESTS

In his essay "On Providence," Seneca quotes the Cynic philosopher Demetrius as saying, "Nothing seems to me more unhappy than the man who has no experience of adversity." Consequently, he says, a wise man will welcome a degree of adversity into his life. He will regard this adversity as a kind of training exercise and might even take delight in it, "just as brave soldiers delight in warfare." Not only that, but in the absence of adversity, a wise man will become restless. "Some men," he says, "have presented themselves of their own accord to misfortune when it is slow to afflict them, seeking to find an opportunity for their worth to shine out when it is in danger of falling into obscurity."[1] This may sound strange, but a wise man knows that although adversity can crush us, it can also, if we are in the right frame of mind, strengthen us and thereby enhance our ability to withstand adversity.

Once we start thinking of setbacks as Stoic tests, we may

discover that instead of dreading them, we look forward to them. Besides giving us a chance to develop our skill in dealing with them, setbacks give us an opportunity to display the skill we have thus far developed. Much as a tennis player can take pride in her playing ability, we can take pride in our ability, when set back, to find a good workaround without becoming angry, anxious, or despondent. It is a wonderful skill to possess—and one that relatively few people do possess.

A tennis player will work hard training for games. She will spend hours in strength and fitness training, doing drills, and playing practice matches, all so she will be at the top of her game when she sets foot on the court for a real match. In similar fashion, you can train for life's setbacks. The training consists in dealing with what might be thought of as practice setbacks, but clarification is in order.

For an event to count as a *setback*, in the strict sense of the word, we can't know that it is going to take place. It's true that we can *inadvertently* set ourselves back—by forgetting to put gas in the car before we get onto the freeway, for example—but we can't set ourselves back *on purpose*, since setbacks require the element of surprise. What we can do, however, is put ourselves into circumstances in which challenging surprises are likely to occur.

If we choose to spend a quiet weekend at home, it is possible, but rather unlikely, that we will experience a setback; if we do, it is likely to be minor, like discovering we're out of shampoo. If we instead choose to spend that weekend taking a twenty-mile hike through a wilderness area, we are likely to experience a number of interesting setbacks. Consequently, going on a hike can count as a form of setback training, with the setbacks we experience counting as practice setbacks. By dealing with them, we can improve our skill at coming up with workarounds, and at staying calm as we do so.

ONE OF THE BEST WAYS to "study for" Stoic tests is to embark on what I am going to call a *Stoic adventure*. In such an adventure, we go out of our way to put ourselves into challenging circumstances—circumstances, that is, in which we are likely to be unpleasantly surprised.

Since different people have different life experiences, what counts as a challenge will vary from person to person. For someone who has led a pampered existence, an adventure might involve doing without, for a time, the people who normally take care of her. For her, making breakfast might count as an adventure. For Michael Jordan, it was an adventure to step away from his career as one of the greatest basketball players in history in order to become, for a time, a minor-league baseball player. And for the Moroccan-born French comedian Gad Elmaleh, it was an adventure to move to America and try to do stand-up comedy—in English.

A Stoic adventurer, in the sense I have in mind, might try to acquire a new skill. Some of the adventures I undertook on becoming a Stoic were to take banjo lessons and a course in Italian. I later used these adventures as the basis for new adventures: I gave a banjo recital, and I traveled to Italy. Each adventure presented me with its own challenges and affected my life in surprising ways.

One of my most consequential adventures after becoming a Stoic, though, was learning how to row. I am at present a serious rower, in the sense that I do something connected with rowing almost every day. I have also become a competitive rower, in the sense that I enter regattas in which I compete against other rowers. That said, I should add that I am not a very good rower. I have the wrong body type for rowing, and to be good at it, I would have to train twice as hard—at least!—as I do.

But for me, failing to win races—or even coming in last place in a race—isn't an issue. My primary objective in rowing is to acquire mettle, not medals. By rowing, I study for Stoic tests. When I am rowing—and even more, when I am racing—unpredictable things happen. An oar might pop out of an oarlock, threatening to capsize my boat. At the start of a race, a passing motorboat might make a wake that partially fills my boat with water, making it even harder to row. And in the sprint to the finish line, another rower might cut in front of me, thereby testing my ability to remain calm and find a workaround, even though I am gasping for air.

ANOTHER ADVANTAGE OF ROWING is that it puts me into intimate contact with what I call *Lazy Bill*.[2] This creature lives in my subconscious mind, where it spends most of its time sleeping.

When I am rowing, though, it routinely puts in an appearance. I will be straining to do a 500-meter practice sprint, or I will be 3,000 meters into a 5,000-meter race, and Lazy Bill will speak up: "You know, Bill, you could just stop rowing. Think of how much better you would feel if you just stopped rowing!"

It is a voice that on many occasions has seduced me. Most of the time, though, I respond to it by rowing even harder: *I'll show you!* Subsequently, I might focus my attention on the number of strokes I have left to complete whatever piece I am rowing and count them off, stroke by stroke. I know that the key to success is to take one more stroke, and then, when I have finished it, take another. By doing this, I can silence and even humiliate Lazy Bill: "You lose, Billy Boy!"

At this point, a word of caution is in order. It is one thing to trash-talk your lazy self, since it is too lazy to do anything about it, but it might be unwise to trash-talk the Stoic gods. Maybe this is just superstition on my part, but then again, they are not only incredibly powerful but are also on the lookout for mortals who are getting bumptious. Best not to take chances.

In daily life, there are many occasions when I could make things easier—in the short run, at least—if I would, metaphorically speaking, "just stop rowing." But I have found that the achievement of significant goals generally requires me to be able and willing to "take one more stroke," even though I am dead tired. I'm convinced that it is this ability, as much as any, that allows some people to excel in the challenges they undertake, while other people fail. It is also possible that at some point in my life, my ability to survive will depend on whether I have the fortitude to take just one more breath—and then another. I would like to think that rowing helps me develop this fortitude.

A spectator at a regatta would naturally think that I am rowing against the other rowers. From my Stoic point of view, though, the other rowers are my teammates in a much more important undertaking: my battle against Lazy Bill. I have nothing against winning a race, in the conventional sense of the word, by rowing faster than the other boats that have entered. What really matters to me, though, is that I soundly defeat Lazy Bill.

I am probably not alone in having a lazy self lurking within me; indeed, it is conceivable that you, dear reader, have one as well. In the coming days, be on the lookout for this being, and when it appears, don't simply capitulate, but consider your options. Experiment with ignoring or even reprimanding it. And ask yourself whether you really want this lowly creature, who has never accomplished *anything* worthy of note, running your life.

Some readers will be baffled by the foregoing discussion. "What do you mean by my 'lazy self'?" they will ask. The readers in question will be unable to remember ever having encountered such a being.

Perhaps it is because they have never done anything physically or mentally challenging enough to wake up their lazy self. Or perhaps they are so used to capitulating to its demands that they no longer regard it as an "other" being. Their lazy self has merged with their true self—or should we say, displaced it? Consequently, doing what their lazy self says doesn't, for them, count as an attack of laziness; it is just life as they know it. How sad!

Although we can't exterminate our lazy self, we can take steps to limit its control over us. We can, in particular, go out of our way to do things that we find physically or mentally exhausting. This will likely awaken our lazy self, and when it appears, we can slap it down, thereby showing it who is in charge of our life. Yes, confronting our lazy self will require unpleasant effort on our part, but the Stoics would argue that this is a small price to pay in defense of our autonomy.

BY EMBARKING ON STOIC ADVENTURES, you can imbue your life with a heroic aspect, in the sense that the author Joseph Campbell had in mind. The hero's journey, Campbell wrote, begins with life in the ordinary world, when along comes the call to adventure. In many cases, the call is refused, and the person remains in the ordinary world. But if the call is accepted, he crosses into a special world in which he experiences tests and ordeals—what I call setbacks. If he meets these challenges, he will return to the ordinary world as a transformed being.

Start undertaking Stoic adventures, and you might notice a change in yourself. Formerly when you encountered a setback, you would have responded with feelings of frustration or anger. Now you might experience a little burst of delight: *Ahhh! A setback to work on!* And if you successfully pass the Stoic test in question, you might experience a deep sense of satisfaction.

It is, as I have said, no small feat to beat the Stoic gods at their own game.

One side effect of studying for Stoic tests is that your self-confidence will rise. The more challenges you successfully meet, the more confident you will become of your ability to meet them. By voluntarily dealing with setbacks, you can also improve your ability to spot the silver linings in the gray clouds of daily life, and appreciate just how relatively setback-free your life is.

CHAPTER 12

EMBRACING "FAILURE"

B ecause people hate to fail, they are reluctant to admit having done so. Consequently, they conceal their failures not only from other people but from themselves. This is unfortunate, since by not acknowledging a failure, they fail to learn from it, and one failure thereby becomes two.

One way to avoid failure is to spend time and energy anticipating obstacles that can be sidestepped. There is, however, a second, far easier way to avoid failure: make a point of choosing only goals that are easy to attain. Using this strategy, though, will make it almost impossible for us to achieve notable success. Indeed, when we examine the lives of accomplished individuals, we find almost without exception that they pursued goals that were difficult to attain, experienced many failures trying to attain them, and nevertheless pressed on.

This is true in the world of technology. The British inventor James Dyson spent fifteen years developing and rejecting more than five thousand vacuum designs in order to perfect his Dual Cyclone vacuum cleaner. It went on sale in 1993 and was a phenomenal success, transforming the very concept of a vacuum cleaner.

It is true in the world of literature. Margaret Mitchell's *Gone with the Wind* was rejected by thirty-eight publishers before becoming one of the best-selling books of the twentieth century, and Robert Pirsig's best-selling *Zen and the Art of Motorcycle Maintenance* was rejected by 121 publishers before seeing the light of day. (And in case you are wondering: yes, the book you are now reading was rejected multiple times before finding a home.)

It is true in the world of art. Vincent Van Gogh painted 860 canvases, only one of which sold during his lifetime. His "failed" paintings are now among the best-loved and most expensive around.

It is true even in the world of mathematics. The English mathematician Andrew Wiles spent seven years trying to prove Fermat's Last Theorem. When the breakthrough idea finally came to him, he publicly announced it, only to discover a mistake in his proof. Some mathematicians would have been crushed by this event, but Wiles managed to find a mathematical workaround and thereby bounced back.

Failure would appear to be an essential ingredient of success in the entrepreneurial world. Howard Schultz of Starbucks coffeehouse fame spoke to 242 people in an attempt to raise money to expand Il Giornale, the precursor to Starbucks.[1] He says that doing cold-call sales for Xerox taught him how to hear no and keep going.

Kathryn Minshew says that raising startup funding for the Muse, a career development platform, meant having to deal with "a no over breakfast, a no over a 10:30 a.m. coffee, a no over lunch, disinterest at 2 p.m., somebody who left a meeting early at 4, and then I would go to drinks and feel like I was being laughed out of the room." She had to endure 148 noes to get to a yes.[2]

Abby Falik is the founder of Global Citizen Year, a not-for-profit organization that sends students abroad for a year of international service between high school and college. She is not only tolerant of hearing noes but is thankful for their existence: "The noes are actually a gift," she says. Her mentor, she explains, had instructed her to "go out into the world and gather as many noes as you possibly can. It is your homework to be rejected over and over and over and over, and then come back and report on it." It was, she said, "the most important thing I could have ever done and the most important advice I could have been given."[3] She learned to listen closely to the noes and to mine them for clues. It turns out that noes are a valuable commodity, if you can tolerate hearing them and know what to do with them.

In the rapidly evolving tech industry, failure can be thought of as a key ingredient in product development. Facebook founder Mark Zuckerberg knows this as well as anyone, and as a result his advice to employees is not "Don't fail," but "Fail faster." They need to forge boldly ahead in their design of a new product, make mistakes, and learn from them so they can go on to make new, better mistakes and ultimately produce successful products.

Failure is also essential to the development of new drugs. Researchers typically spend more than a decade trying and rejecting very many drugs before finding one that meets the FDA's standards for safety and efficacy. In an attempt to keep his researchers' morale high in the midst of all this failure, Severin Schwan, CEO of Roche Holding AG, gives champagne lunches to honor research teams whose drug development efforts came up dry. His thinking: "I would argue, from a cultural point of view, it's more important to praise the people for the nine times they fail than for the one time they succeed." [4]

At this point, readers with Stoical leanings might suggest that our goal in life should be, not to become rich and famous like Schultz and Zuckerberg, but to live a tranquil life, one in which we experience as few negative emotions and as much delight as possible. I quite agree with this suggestion, but two observations are in order. First, as the lives of Seneca and Marcus Aurelius demonstrate, it is possible to achieve "worldly success" while practicing Stoicism. And second, even if we think people like Schultz and Zuckerberg are pursuing the wrong goals, we can nevertheless gain important insights by examining the manner in which they pursue them. They have the ability to try something, fail, learn, and try again. Maybe they were born with these abilities, but more likely they acquired a failure-response strategy that would let them take their failures in stride. Let us now turn our attention to one such strategy.

Suppose your goal is to succeed at some challenging undertaking. You need to go into it fully realizing that you will likely experience lots of failure. You can substantially reduce the sting of this failure—and thereby increase your chance of eventual success—by engaging in a bit of creative framing: you can, in particular, think of your failures as *obstacles* rather than *setbacks*.

To better appreciate this distinction, consider obstacle races. In many of them, athletes are given a map showing the course and its obstacles. At one point, they might have to climb a wall; at another, crawl through a pipe; and at yet another, use a rope to swing across a ditch full of water. Since they know full well the obstacles that lie in wait, it is incorrect to describe them as *setbacks*, in the strict sense of the word. There is, after all, no element of surprise in encountering them. From a racer's point of view, cutting a hand while climbing the wall might count as a setback, but encountering the wall itself doesn't. This distinction between setbacks and obstacles may sound like a quibble, but as we have seen, how we frame a setback has a very real impact on our chances of successfully overcoming it.

Suppose you decide to undertake a personally significant challenge—say, to graduate from college. You can treat your education as the academic equivalent of an obstacle course, and as part of your planning, you can map out the obstacles that lie ahead. You will have to take certain courses, each of which will have its own obstacles: there will be classes to attend, notes to take, readings to do, tests to take, and papers to write. And within these obstacles, there will be yet other obstacles. To write a paper, for example, the first obstacle will be to conduct some research, the next will be to construct an outline, and so on. To prepare for an exam, the first obstacle will be to gather the relevant notes and the second will be to absorb the content of those notes.

To many people, the goal of graduating from college seems daunting. This is part of the reason why in the United States, only one in three people over age twenty-five has accomplished it. To make the dream of becoming a college graduate achievable, it helps to deconstruct your macro-goal of graduating into a long list of mini-goals, such as passing certain classes, that you in turn deconstruct into very long lists of micro-goals, such as completing certain assignments.

The key thing is that each of these micro-goals is eminently doable. Yes, achieving them will require some intelligence, but it is mostly a matter of self-discipline: you've just got to make yourself invest the necessary effort. In other words, to accomplish your macro-goal of becoming a college graduate, you don't need to be a heroic genius; you need only be clever and persistent. You need only do the academic equivalent of taking "one more stroke" in a rowing race.

Similarly, in the business world, you can deconstruct the

macro-goal of raising funds for a startup into mini-goals and micro-goals. Think again about Abby Falik, who went out into the world expecting to hear noes, the way runners at the starting line of the 400-meter hurdle race expect to encounter hurdles. On encountering them, she didn't become despondent. To the contrary, hearing a no meant that she was making progress in the project her mentor had assigned her—namely, to collect noes.

There is, of course, a chance that despite your best efforts, you don't accomplish the macro-goal of the challenge you've undertaken. If this happens, you needn't hang your head in shame. After all, you did your best, and what more can you do than that? You should also keep in mind that there is something much, much worse than failing to do something difficult, and that is not even attempting to do it because you feared failure.

CHAPTER 13

TOUGHNESS TRAINING

Expanding Your Comfort Zone

Most setbacks are easily avoided. Simply by checking your car's fuel gauge, for example, you can avoid running out of gas on the freeway. Likewise, by checking the weather report before embarking on a walk, you can avoid getting caught in the rain without an umbrella. Another thing you can do to avoid setbacks is learn more about how the world works. Someone who has taken the time to learn how computers work, or how a particular application works, will likely experience far fewer setbacks than someone who hasn't. When her computer "acts up," she will know how to fix the problem.

We have, however, another, rather less obvious way to decrease the number of setbacks we experience. For an event to count as a setback, it must not only come as a surprise to us but must, from our point of view, count as a change for the worse. Besides taking steps to avoid being surprised by undesirable events, Stoics recommend that we take steps to change what, for us, counts as an undesirable event. This suggestion sounds farfetched, I realize, so allow me to explain.

Suppose a couple are driving to the airport on a hot summer day. Halfway there, the car's air conditioner stops working, and the temperature inside the car soars. For the husband, the heat is no big deal: because he is a geologist, he is accustomed to being out in the sun. His wife, though, is a computer programmer who spends her days in a climate-controlled office. She breaks into a sweat and before long starts complaining. For her, the air conditioner malfunction is a significant and unforeseen change for the worse, so for her, it counts as a setback.

Fast-forward, and suppose the couple have taken their seats in a plane. The wife is now considerably more comfortable than she was in the car. The cabin of the airplane is, after all, a climate-controlled environment. Meanwhile her husband has broken into a cold sweat, because he has an intense fear of flying. Whereas the discomfort his wife experienced in the car was physical, his is emotional, but it is nevertheless very real and is in many respects worse than hers. As the plane rolls out onto the runway, his wife holds his hand and says reassuring things, with little effect. He expresses his anger about having to take such a trip and swears that he will never, ever fly again.

This tale illustrates something we all know: different people have different comfort zones. Some have very broad zones and can therefore feel comfortable in a wide range of circumstances: we might even be surprised to hear them express discomfort. Other people are uncomfortable unless everything is just so.

For whatever reason, these hard-to-please individuals often feel a need to tell others about their discomfort. They want the rest of us to be aware of it and ideally to do something about it. Suppose that in an attempt to please them, we turn on the air conditioning in the room that they say is too hot. They might now complain that the air conditioner is too noisy. Their lives must be difficult—as are the lives of those who have to deal with them on a daily basis.

WHY DO WE HAVE the comfort zones we do? And why do different people have different-sized zones? You might think it is a consequence of our genetic makeup, and to some extent it is. To a much greater extent, though, our life experience determines the size and shape of our comfort zone. In particular, if we make a point of exposing ourselves to things that make us either physically or emotionally uncomfortable, we can train ourselves to be comfortable with them and thereby expand our comfort zone.

The ancient Stoics realized this and made comfort zone expansion—let us refer to it as *toughness training*—part of their Stoic practice.[1] They made a point of periodically going out of their way to do things that made them uncomfortable. This may sound masochistic, but the Stoics knew that exposure to discomfort, if done in a systematic fashion, would have the effect of reducing the total amount of discomfort they experienced in daily living. It was therefore a good investment of their time and energy.

Before I go any further, let me clarify the difference between toughness training and Stoic adventures (see Chapter 11). We undertake Stoic adventures, such as trying to climb a mountain, so we can experience setbacks—so we can, in other words, be surprised by unpleasant events. The Stoics knew that by doing this, we would sharpen our setback-response reflexes. Then, when we experienced a setback in daily living, we would, instead of getting frustrated or angry, simply label it a Stoic test and calmly set about trying to find the optimal workaround for it. By undertaking Stoic adventures, then, we are studying for the Stoic tests that life is likely to administer.

When we engage in toughness training, by contrast, we aren't *hoping for* our circumstances to take an unexpected turn for the worse. To the contrary, we are going out of our way to *make* them take a turn for the worse, so we can expand our comfort zone. In toughness training, in its purest form, there is zero element of surprise.

That said, it is possible to combine toughness training with Stoic adventures. Suppose you contemplate climbing a 4,000-meter mountain as an adventure, in the expectation that the climb will present you with setbacks to deal with. Suppose, too, that you know from past experience that you are affected by altitude sickness when you climb mountains this high. For you, the adventure of climbing the mountain will therefore also count as toughness training. The ancient Stoics were fine with this two-for-the-price-of-one phenomenon; indeed, they might have quipped that the fact that we can study for Stoic tests while doing toughness training is proof that the Stoic gods love us and want us to thrive.

I should also clarify the difference between toughness training and the practice of negative visualization (see Chapter 6). Negative visualization involves *thinking about how* things could be worse; toughness training involves *causing* things to be worse. In negative visualization, we might imagine that we have nothing to eat for lunch. *What would that feel like?* we will wonder. If we voluntarily skip lunch as part of our toughness training, we won't simply *wonder* what it feels like to have nothing to eat; we will *find out*, and we will also find out that missing a meal is an utterly survivable event, which in turn will increase our self-confidence.

YOUR COMFORT ZONE HAS TWO DIMENSIONS, one physical and the other emotional, and your goal in toughness training should be to expand both of them.

To become emotionally tougher, you need to tackle your fears—you need, in other words, to deal with what we might think of as your scared self. (For the record, your scared self lives in your subconscious mind, next door to your lazy self.) You can do this by going out of your way to expose yourself, in measured doses, to the things you fear.[2] If, for example, you have a fear of public speaking, part of your toughness training can be to seek out opportunities to appear before small and friendly audiences. When you feel comfortable doing this, you can move on to larger audiences. As a result of this desensitization process, you might someday, much to your amazement, find yourself standing fearlessly before an audience of hundreds of people.

For evidence that this remedy for emotional discomfort is effective, consider the things you can do without a second thought. At a swimming pool, you might fearlessly dive from the diving board, but think back on all the fears you had to overcome in order to feel comfortable doing this. You first had to get accustomed to being in the shallow end of the pool without holding your parent's hand. After that, you had to get accustomed to swimming in the deep end by yourself; then to jumping into the swimming pool from the deck; then to diving in headfirst from the deck; then to jumping in from the diving board; and finally to diving in from the diving board. At each of these steps, you would have experienced fear, and at each step, the fear would have dissipated after a few repetitions.

Do you remember, the first time you drove a car, how scary it was? And do you remember the first time you parallel-parked a car? And now you do these things without a second thought. You may even do them while simultaneously checking your e-mail on your cell phone—which behavior, I should add, is not advisable.

They say familiarity breeds contempt. This may or may not be true, but it is clear that familiarity breeds *comfort*: do something scary often enough, and it not only ceases to be scary, it becomes automatic. Some readers may not be able to relate to the above examples, for the simple reason that their fears prevented them from learning how to drive or swim. For these readers, yet another Stoic challenge is in order: start your toughness training by dealing with these fears. In other words, toughen yourself up by taking driving or swimming lessons.

YOUR TOUGHNESS TRAINING, besides being concerned with things that make you *emotionally* uncomfortable, will be concerned with *physical* discomfort. In the summer, your training might require spending time outside in the heat even though you could instead spend it in an air-conditioned room. In winter, it might mean not just spending your time out in the cold but underdressing for that weather. As part of my own toughness training, for example, I make a point of allowing myself to be a bit chilly in October: I go out in shirtsleeves, while those around me are wearing sweaters. I have found that by doing this, I will be comfortably warm when January rolls around, even though I am wearing just a sweater while those around me are bundled up in multiple layers of clothing—but still seem cold.

Your toughness training can extend to your diet. You can try skipping between-meal snacks and cutting down portion sizes at meals. Yes, you will feel hungry, but this will give you an opportunity to explore hunger, maybe for the first time in your life.[3] As a result of this exploration, you will likely make some interesting discoveries. One is that your body will get used to the new eating regimen, so that even though you eat less food, you experience less hunger than you did before. It might then dawn on you that what you previously thought of as hunger wasn't biological hunger at all; it was instead a psychological mélange of boredom and discontent.

The dietary component of your toughness training might have a silver lining, in the form of weight loss. You might also discover that your meals are more deeply satisfying than they were before.

Your toughness training should have an exercise component. Its form will obviously depend on how fit you currently are, as well as on your age and health. For some people, it might involve walking around the block; for others, it might involve running for miles. When you begin your program, you will likely find that it causes you a degree of physical discomfort, not only while you are exercising but after your workout has ended. You might feel tired for the rest of the day, and the next day you might be sore.

It might, at this point, seem that your toughness training, rather than making you more comfortable, is having just the opposite effect. You need to keep in mind, though, that the goal of toughness training is not to let you live in uninterrupted comfort. It is to expand your comfort zone so you remain comfortable in a wider range of circumstances. This expansion has a price tag, in terms of discomfort, but on the whole, the comfort you gain will outweigh this cost.

In particular, if you stick with your exercise program, you will discover not only that your exercise-induced soreness goes away, but that you are, on the whole, more comfortable than you used to be. Before you began your program, you might have gotten winded taking walks or climbing stairs; now you feel a spring in your step as you move around. You will also find it emotionally reassuring to know that because of your training, your body is better suited to deal with any physically challenging circumstances that you might encounter.

AS YOU TOUGHEN UP, you can intensify your training—assuming, of course, that there are no health risks in doing so. If you walk to get exercise, for example, you can include segments of fast walking or even running in your workouts. If you are running, you can increase the distance, or experiment with doing sprints. Likewise, you can intensify the dietary component of your toughness training by experimenting with fasting. At first you can try skipping single meals, then move on to going an entire day without food. As a result of this training, you will become confident of your ability to deal with emergency situations. In particular, if unforeseen circumstances force you to miss a meal, you will be fine, inasmuch as you will simply be doing involuntarily something you have done voluntarily on many occasions.

Your advanced toughness training can extend to your lifestyle. You can dramatically simplify your way of living for a time. Seneca, one of the richest men in Rome, would periodically "practice poverty." He advised the rest of us to follow his example by setting aside "a number of days during which you will be content with the plainest of food, and very little of it, and with rough, coarse clothing, and will ask yourself, 'Is this what one used to dread?' "[4]

Whereas Seneca advocated that we set aside periods to live as if we were poor, Musonius Rufus, the Stoic philosopher who handled so well his banishment to Gyaros (see Chapter 4), thought we should *always* live simply. At mealtimes, he said, we should learn to be satisfied with sensible amounts of simple foods. Our clothing should also be simple, and when we choose our dwelling place, we need to keep in mind that its primary purpose is to shelter us from the weather, as well as to keep out excessive heat and cold—needs that can be met, he adds, by living in a small cave.[5]

Regardless of whether you practice poverty or choose merely to live simply, you should make a point of looking for the sources of delight that remain available to you. If the day is clear, be sure to notice the sky: it didn't have to be blue, but it is, and isn't that wonderful? And if you are indoors, be sure to appreciate the smiles on the faces of the people you encounter. Those smiles are a wonderful gift that is all too easy to take for granted.

As you collect sources of delight, you might experience what I call *meta-delight*—you might, that is, take delight in your ability to take delight in such things. Seneca was aware of this phenomenon: "Barley porridge, or a crust of barley bread, and water do not make a very cheerful diet, but nothing gives one keener pleasure than the ability to derive pleasure even from that."[6]

BEFORE ENDING THIS DISCUSSION of toughness training, some additional clarification is in order. The training exercises I have described may sound like acts of self-denial performed by adherents of exotic religions, but there is an important difference. In most cases, religious ascetics deny themselves pleasures and subject themselves to various discomforts so they can experience a better *afterlife*. God, they think, will be impressed by their seriousness and consequently will reward them with a heavenly eternity. By contrast, Stoics engage in toughness training so they can have a better *life*.

The ancient Stoics obviously weren't hedonists. Their goal was not to maximize the amount of pleasure they experienced; it was to attain and maintain tranquility. But suppose you told a Stoic that after considering your philosophical options, you decided not to join him but instead to become a full-out hedonist: you were going to live for pleasure.

Even then, the Stoics would advise you to engage in toughness training. This is because, as strange as it may seem, experiencing too much comfort will reduce your capacity for experiencing pleasure. As Seneca put it, "When mind and body have been corrupted by pleasure, nothing seems bearable—not because the things which you suffer are hard, but because you are soft."[7] Toughness training will also intensify whatever pleasures you do experience. If you spend the morning out in the cold as part of your training, the warmth you experience when you come in will be delicious. Eat ice cream every day, and if it is good ice cream, it will be satisfying; eat ice cream only a few times a year, though, and it will be so incredibly delicious that you might find yourself pitying those who, if only they were less hedonistic, could experience this level of pleasure.

CHAPTER 14

SETUPS

When Things Take an
Unexpected Turn for the Better

S ometimes life goes smoothly: the setbacks we encounter are few and easily overcome. This, we might tell ourselves, is how things should always be. Once we start thinking in terms of Stoic tests, though, we will respond to such periods with mixed emotions. We might grumble that they deprive us of chances to "show our Stoic stuff"—a concern we can deal with by undertaking Stoic adventures. Such a period might also make us nervous: we will worry that the Stoic gods are setting us up—that they have arranged this setback-free period to set the stage for a particularly devious Stoic test. Allow me to explain.

I've mentioned that I'm a rower—not a very good one, but a committed rower nonetheless. I compete at the masters level, but this statement is potentially misleading. To compete as a masters rower, a person needn't demonstrate a mastery of rowing; he need only be old. To level the playing field, masters rowers are assigned an age-dependent time handicap. As I write this, my handicap is thirty-eight seconds. This means a "young" person—someone who is, say, twenty-eight—will have to do a 1,000-meter race in thirty-eight fewer seconds than I do in order for us to tie, in age-adjusted terms. Next year, my handicap will be up to forty seconds. I can hardly wait.

Because of handicapping, the person who crosses the finish line first in a masters race won't necessarily win. Rowers' handicaps have to be subtracted from their elapsed time in order to come up with their age-adjusted time, and the rower with the best age-adjusted time will be declared the winner. It is therefore possible for a very old rower, although the last to cross the finish line, to be declared the winner. Likewise, the person who crosses the finish line first, if he is young, might come in last place, in age-adjusted terms.

A few years ago I rowed in a 1,000-meter race against a competitive field. I rowed well: I followed my race plan and didn't make any big mistakes. I successfully fended off Lazy Bill, who put in a dramatic appearance 700 meters into the race, with repeated entreaties to "slow down, for God's sake!" After completing the race, I docked my boat and carried it back to the trailer. A few minutes later the results of the race were announced over the venue's PA system. I had won! I went off to collect my gold medal, and on being handed it, I felt the rush of success. It was wonderful.

I came back to my team's trailer proudly wearing the medal and eager to show it to my teammates. I described my race-winning strategy to anyone who would listen—how I'd struggled during the last 300 meters, and how I'd thought my heart would explode during the last five strokes. I told them that yes, it would be okay if they took my picture wearing the medal. And then the PA system crackled back to life. It informed us that there had been a mistake in the previous announcement. The names of the top three finishers were read, and mine was not among them.

I went to the scoring tent to find out what was going on. It turned out that race officials had accidentally given me an extra minute of age handicap, and once that was removed, I had fallen from first place to last. *Groan!* I was stunned, but then it dawned on me that I had been the target of a setup.

In the *setbacks* we have examined in this book, the Stoic gods place an unexpected obstruction in our path; in a *setup*, they are extraordinarily nice to us, but only in order to set the stage for a subsequent setback. In this case, they created in me the perception that I had won a race that I had in fact lost. By doing so, they made the setback I subsequently experienced that much worse. It involved an element of (self-inflicted) public humiliation. It also revealed a streak of Stoic hypocrisy in me: after all my talk about how I race as a form of Stoic training, here I was, boasting about my victory. *Blush!*

I did my best to regain my equanimity. After returning the medal, I congratulated the Stoic gods for their ingenuity and went back to my team's trailer. I explained the timing error to my teammates and lightened things with a touch of self-deprecating humor. "The next time I win a race," I told them, "I'm not going off to collect the medal. I'm going to the timing tent to demand a recount!"

THE ANCIENT GREEKS were well aware of the setup phenomenon. They believed that the goddess Nemesis liked to punish extreme pride and foolish overconfidence, otherwise known as hubris. What particularly irked her were people who not only *expected* things to go well for them in the future but also were convinced that they somehow *deserved* for them to go well. When she discovered such individuals, she would waste no time bringing them back to reality. How dare they think they were immune to setbacks! They were, after all, mere mortals. Nemesis was both powerful and remorseless, and it was impossible to hide from her. She also had a talent for arranging setups that, besides being brutal, were ironic.

Nemesis is most famous for her punishment of Narcissus, a youth who, because of his good looks, had many admirers, all of whom he spurned. Narcissus can best be described as—you guessed it—*narcissistic*. He was quite in love with himself. Nemesis consequently went into action. She lured him to a pool in which he could see his own reflection. On seeing it, he found his beauty so compelling that he could not tear himself away and as a result starved to death.

On another occasion, it dawned on the tyrannical king Polycrates that his life was going exceedingly well. He started worrying that Nemesis would take notice and punish him for his good fortune. To assuage her, he made numerous offerings, but his string of good luck continued. Desperate, Polycrates sailed out into the ocean and threw his most valuable ring into the water as an offering to Nemesis.

Convinced that this would do the job, he sailed back home and decreed that a giant feast be held. His cook ordered that hundreds of fish be caught so they could be served at the feast. The cook cleaned the fish, but when he opened the belly of the largest one, he found the ring Polycrates had thrown into the sea. It was a sure sign, Polycrates thought, that Nemesis had rejected his offering. He became so anxious that he couldn't eat, and like Narcissus, he perished.

The Roman Stoics were well aware of the danger presented by a period that was free of setbacks. Seneca warned that "Although all things in excess bring harm, the greatest danger comes from excessive good fortune: it stirs the brain, invites the mind to entertain idle fancies, and shrouds in thick fog the distinction between falsehood and truth."[1] When such a period ends, as it someday surely will, the setback that ends it will seem much worse than it otherwise would.

AS WE HAVE SEEN, the ancient Stoics weren't opposed to the experience of positive emotions, such as delight and even joy. They cautioned, though, against allowing ourselves to become overjoyed, since doing so increases our chances of being miserable when we are ultimately set back. We should instead take good fortune in stride, the way, ideally, we take bad fortune. Do things right, and other people will be unaware of our fortune, whether it be good or bad. Obviously, I did not follow this advice on "winning" the above-described race. Shame on me. And have I learned my lesson? I hope so, but only time will tell.

Some will reject the advice that we keep our good news to ourselves. They are convinced that we should share our successes with friends and relatives, and that doing so brings our joy into their lives. This *can* happen, but it is also possible for people to respond in a negative manner to our good news. Suppose, in particular, that as the result of our successes, we start getting cocky, as if this is simply the way things are supposed to be. On detecting such an attitude, friends and relatives are likely to start rooting against us, albeit secretly. They don't think that we are better, harder working, or more deserving than they are; we are just lucky, and here we are, flaunting our luck before them.

Suppose that even though we don't publicize our successes, other people become aware of them. Our socially safest response, under these circumstances, is to attribute our success to luck. It is probably what people already think, so we won't get an argument from them. It also makes them less likely to become unwitting accomplices in the Stoic gods' eventual attempt to take us down a notch.

In Chapter 6 we encountered Daniel Kahneman, who together with Amos Tversky did pioneering research on anchoring and framing. In 2011 Kahneman wrote a general audience book describing their research, *Thinking, Fast and Slow*. He worried that doing this would damage his professional reputation—professors aren't supposed to write books (like the one you are now reading) that "normal people" can understand and profit from. But he went ahead and published it anyway. *Thinking, Fast and Slow* soon made the *New York Times* best-seller list.

Astonished, Kahneman sheepishly explained to his colleagues that the book's appearance there was a mistake. When it stubbornly remained on the list, Kahneman modified his story: he told people that it was staying on the list only so that the *Times* wouldn't have to admit to having made a mistake in putting it there in the first place.[2] It was a clever envy avoidance maneuver on his part.

CHAPTER 15

DEATH

Your Exit Exam

L ike it or not, you are going to die. Stoics therefore advise you, even though you may be young and in perfect health, to contemplate your death. Let us explore some of the forms this contemplation can take.

In Chapter 6 we encountered the negative visualization technique. In a typical visualization exercise, you imagine—and even try to visualize—not having something that you in fact have, such as your lunch, your home, or your spouse. You don't, as we have seen, dwell on the possibility of losing these things; you simply allow yourself to have a flickering thought about it. The whole process requires minimal mental effort and takes only a few seconds. Using this technique will temporarily curb your tendency to take the elements of your daily existence for granted and will thereby enhance your ability to take delight in the life you happen to be living.

As a meditation on death, you could try to imagine what it

would be like to lose not your job or your spouse but your very existence. This, however, is impossible to do: if you have ceased to exist, there is no one left to experience what it is like to be dead. You could alternatively imagine what the world would be like if you had never been born, but this would be mere speculation on your part, unless you had the assistance of someone like Clarence Odbody—the fictional angel, second class, from the 1946 movie *It's a Wonderful Life*. Fortunately, there are variants of the negative visualization technique that can play an important role in your death meditations.

One is what might be called *last-time meditation*, in which you acknowledge that because you are mortal, there will be a last time for everything you do. There will be a last time you flip a light switch, a last time you eat dinner, and a last time you say goodbye to your parents, spouse, children, and friends. You have already done some things for the last time: there is a very good chance, for example, that you will never again dial a rotary telephone, type on a typewriter, or take a math exam. There will be a last time you lay your head on a pillow, as well as a last time you take a breath.

To last-time meditate, you periodically pause in your daily routine to reflect that no matter what you are doing, there is a chance that this is the last time you will ever do it. Indeed, there is an off chance that this book is the last one you will ever read, and even that this very sentence is the last you will read—although I sincerely hope you not only finish the remaining sentences of this book but go on to have a long and happy life thereafter. These last-time meditations may sound depressing, but they have the power to infuse everyday occurrences with meaning.

Another variant of negative visualization involves what might be called *prospective retrospection*. To employ this technique, you periodically pause, as you are going about your daily routine, to reflect on the likelihood that at some point in the future, you will wish you could travel back in time to *this very moment*. You may be doing something mundane, like driving to the store to buy food to cook for dinner. Live long enough, though, and you might someday find yourself wishing that you could again perform this utterly prosaic task.

Suppose you successfully avoid death for many decades, and as a result your children place you in a nursing home. Sitting there, with a television blaring in the far corner of the commons room, you might find yourself longing for the good old days when you still had a car to drive and were fit enough to cook yourself dinner. Those days will seem like a dream world. In doing prospective retrospection, you simply remind yourself that at the present moment, almost regardless of what you are doing, you are quite likely living in the dream world of your future self. Enjoy living that dream!

Some people will interpret these mortality meditations as symptoms of an unhealthy obsession with death, but Stoics would argue just the opposite. In doing these meditations, you are not *dwelling* on death. They are momentary, impromptu exercises, and rather than being depressing, they can be curiously revitalizing.

Many people are bored by or even loathe their daily routine. This is unfortunate, since a life filled with loathed days will end up being a loathed life. By engaging in negative visualization and its variants, you can increase the chance that, instead of simply enduring the moments of your life, you savor them to the greatest extent possible and thereby increase your chances of extracting every drop of delight that your life has to offer. You might find that instead of simply grinding through your allotted days, you embrace and even celebrate the life you find yourself living.

Stoics would even go so far as to assert that you are lucky to be mortal. If you were immortal and knew it, you would be far more likely to take your days for granted. You squandered today? Not to worry, since the immortal you would always have a tomorrow. Acknowledge your mortality, though, and you will be acutely aware that every day you live represents a withdrawal from a life bank that has a finite number of days in it. In most circumstances, you don't know what that number is. It might be as low as 1, meaning that this is your last day alive, but it might also be 25,500, meaning that you have seventy years more to live. Since you have a finite number of days left to you, they are precious, and it would be foolish to waste them.

YOU LIKELY WENT THROUGH EARLY CHILDHOOD oblivious to your own mortality. Then, perhaps in response to the death of a pet, neighbor, or relative, you found out that things die. Sometime after that, it dawned on you that you would also die, but your understanding of your mortality might be described as nebulous and theoretical. Yes, you would die, but it would be sometime in the distant future, likely decades and decades away. This assumption made it possible for you to shove thoughts of death into the back of your mind, maybe even into one of the closets conveniently located there.

Some people never move beyond this level of understanding their mortality. They go to bed young and healthy, the way they have thousands of times before, only to die in their sleep. Most people, though, will at some point in their life be forced to confront their mortality. On a visit to their doctor, for example, they might be informed that they have advanced pancreatic cancer and have only a year of life remaining. Or on the field of battle, they might know, without anyone saying a word, that they have been shot, are losing copious amounts of blood, and have only a few minutes more to live.

When, as a child, you became aware that animals and people die, your parents probably gave you a sugarcoated explanation of death. They might have told you that in dying, your dog Rover didn't cease to exist but went to heaven, where he was quite happy. They said the same of the relatives and neighbors who died. This raised the possibility that you might, when you ultimately joined them in heaven, be treated to the sight of your grandma holding Rover in her lap. Wouldn't that be grand?

Many people never really move on from this childhood conception of death, and it is easy to understand why. Believing in heaven not only takes the sting out of death but potentially makes death something to long for. In heaven, after all, you get to see all the people you loved who parted life ahead of you. You also get a do-over on life. And because heaven is eternal, you don't have to go through that second chance at life fearing the death of your dog, your loved ones, and most significantly, yourself. What could be better?

The prospect of life in heaven raises some important questions. There is scant evidence that we will have a continued existence after our earthly demise, but suppose that such an existence is possible. You might end up spending it not in heaven but in hell. Even if you are a devout Roman Catholic who has done everything that, according to your faith, is necessary to ascend to heaven—indeed, even if you are the pope himself—it might turn out that the earth's 1.8 billion Muslims are right, so you have wasted your time. Conversely, if you are a devout Muslim who has done everything necessary to ascend to heaven—known by them as Jannah or Paradise—the earth's 1.2 billion Roman Catholics may turn out to be right, in which case, too bad for you.

Suppose, for the sake of argument, that you do end up in heaven. As we have seen, it isn't clear that you will live happily ever after there; indeed, retain your earthly tendency to take whatever you have for granted, and you might, before very long, start taking your heavenly existence for granted, and a short time after that, you might start complaining about life in heaven.

Sometimes when I tell people this, they respond by saying they are going to turn over a new leaf when they die and will be very satisfied with their heavenly existence. My question for them: if they have it in their power to become capable of satisfaction, why not use that power while still on earth, thereby making their earthly existence more heavenly than would otherwise be the case?

SUPPOSE YOU CAME TO POSSESS INFORMATION about when and how you will die. What would you do with it? A Stoic would have no trouble answering this question. Since his primary goal in life is to attain and then maintain tranquility, he would spend the time that remained experiencing as few negative emotions as he can, with as little anxiety, fear, anger, and regret as possible. He would do his best to embrace the sources of delight that his life still had to offer. In more general terms, he would regard his dying days as an opportunity to top a good life with a beautiful and fitting capstone.

At the same time, a Stoic will realize that obstacles can arise that make it very difficult for him to have a good death. One such obstacle is extreme pain. A Stoic will be quite adept at preventing negative emotions and in dealing with them if prevention efforts fail. Pain, however, is a sensation, not an emotion, and if it is sufficiently intense, it can undermine his reasoning ability, thereby depriving him of the tools the Stoic gods have given him for dealing with life's challenges. The onset of dementia late in life can likewise strip him of his reasoning ability, resulting in an unfortunate end to what was a very good life.

The goal of remaining tranquil until we die seems eminently

sensible, but how can we accomplish it? We can once again use the Stoic test strategy, only now the challenge we are dealing with will be the loss not of our cell phone, our job, or our freedom, but of our very life. We can think of it as our Stoic exit exam, the test that all the previous Stoic tests have been preparing us for. In Chapter 7 we saw how, through the clever use of framing, we can make everyday setbacks more tolerable. We can likewise employ framing to ease our passage from life.

Like any Stoic test, our Stoic exit exam has two components. The first is to look for a workaround for the setback. If we have received a cancer diagnosis, we should probably get a second opinion and even look into experimental treatments. Likewise, if we have been wounded on the field of battle, we should try to slow the loss of blood in case help arrives. In doing these things, it is important that to the extent possible, we stay calm and focused.

Suppose, however, that our search for a workaround is unsuccessful. Our death, we conclude, is both imminent and unavoidable. We must then turn our attention to a different undertaking: having the best death possible. This is when our Stoic training can come into play.

Consider again the last-time meditation that I discussed earlier in this chapter. When we finally do become aware of the likely time and circumstances of our death, we might find ourselves doing it as part of our daily routine. We will be poignantly aware that the conversations we are having, the meals we are eating, and the kisses we are sharing could be our last. They will therefore have special meaning. Paradoxically, it is possible that in dying, we will be more alive than we have ever been. The prospect of death will, at last, make us fully aware of how beautiful, how wonderful our life is.

In order to have our best chance at a good death, we must keep in mind the Stoic principle that we should not concern ourselves with things we cannot control. Doing so is a waste of time under any circumstances, but doing so in our dying days is a waste of the precious little time we have remaining: rather than fighting our imminent death, we need to embrace it. Many elderly people realize this instinctively and inform those around them that it is their time to go.

Another central principle of Stoicism is that we should be socially useful: we should, that is, do what we can to help those around us have better lives. A Stoic will know that her dying presents a wonderful opportunity for her to encourage others to rethink their way of living. She can remind those around her that inasmuch as they have only one life to live, they are foolish to waste even a moment of it being miserable when they have it in their power to experience delight. And she can simultaneously demonstrate to them, during her last days of life, what it means to have a good death.

LET US END THIS DISCUSSION of death by considering three cases. In 1996 the psychologist Amos Tversky learned that he was dying of metastatic melanoma. He carried on his normal routine, and most of those who encountered him were oblivious to his condition. He died not long afterward, at age fifty-nine. During a discussion of his impending death, he told a friend: "Life is a book. The fact that it was a short book doesn't mean it wasn't a good book. It was a very good book."[1]

Although Tversky died a natural death, he had obtained drugs that would allow him to end his life quickly and painlessly, if he chose to do so. The ancient Stoics would have understood this choice. They thought that under some circumstances, suicide wasn't just morally acceptable; it was sensible. Seneca, for example, imagined God explaining his thinking to us: "I have made nothing easier than dying. I placed life on a downward slope: if it is prolonged, only observe and you will see how short, how easy is the path that leads to freedom."[2] Dying, then, is the easy part of your Stoic exit exam; the challenge is to retain your equanimity. I should add that as long as your continued existence can help others, Stoics would regard it as cowardly to commit suicide.

Let me develop Tversky's life-is-a-book metaphor a bit further. Living your life is like writing a novel that is a curious blend of fiction and nonfiction. Each day you must add another day's events to the manuscript. You have considerable creative freedom with respect to the thoughts, utterances, and actions of the novel's protagonist—yourself. He or she can do anything you are capable of doing. The other aspects of the novel must be utterly realistic, though. It must be set in the present-day actual world, and its characters must be existing people who respond to the protagonist's actions exactly as they would in real life.

Writing a novel that meets these specifications would be challenging enough, but it turns out that there is a complicating factor: your editor refuses to give you a deadline. She can download and publish your manuscript whenever she wants. Maybe she'll do it tomorrow, or maybe she'll wait several decades. The novel's deadline, in other words, will resemble your life's quite literal dead line.

Your goal, under such circumstances, should be to make sure that no matter when your editor publishes your novel, it will stand as a complete work—or as complete as is humanly possible. Yes, some story elements will remain unresolved, but no important business will be left undone. In particular, those who helped you will have been thanked for their help, and the people you love will know of this love. There will be precious few things about the plot that you would want to change, if you had it in your power to do so. This is in part because of the choices you made but also, and more important, because you made it your business to embrace whatever life you found yourself living.

BESIDES FRAMING OUR DEATH AS A TEST, we can frame it as an adventure—indeed, as the last and in many respects the greatest adventure of our life. If we do this, instead of approaching death with dread, we can approach it with anticipation. I know this sounds strange, but the ancient Stoic philosopher Julius Canus apparently succeeded in doing just that.

During his reign, the Roman emperor Caligula condemned

numerous people to death, often for frivolous reasons. Canus was among them. When the centurion came to lead him to his execution, he was playing a board game with another prisoner. He complained not about being taken away to die but about being prevented from finishing the game. He told the centurion not to believe his opponent if he subsequently claimed to have won the game, since Canus had been one piece ahead when his circumstances forced him to retire.[3] This action likely involved a bit of posturing on his part, and yet even two millennia later, it is an impressive bit of philosophical theater.

And how did Canus succeed in taking so much of the sting out of his impending death? By treating it as an adventure. Just before his execution, someone asked him for his thoughts. He replied that he was preparing to observe the moment of death: would his spirit be able to witness its departure from his body? Even though his death would be a fatal setback to his future, he found a way to extract value from it and thereby gave it a silver lining.

The American poet Mary Oliver is winner of both the Pulitzer Prize and the National Book Award. In her poem "When Death Comes," she expresses an outlook on death that resembles that of Canus. She tells us that when death comes—like "an iceberg between the shoulder blades"—she doesn't want to realize, now that it is too late to do anything about it, that she has simply been a visitor in this world. She doesn't want to end up sighing, frightened, or arguing. She wants instead to enter that "cottage of darkness" full of curiosity, knowing that she spent her life playing the role of "a bride married to amazement." Whether Oliver realizes it or not, hers is a Stoic approach to living and dying.

OF THE ANCIENT ROMAN STOICS, Seneca has played the biggest role in this book. He had many insights not only into setbacks but also into death, the final setback. Allow me, then, to end this chapter by describing his death.

The Stoics, as we have seen, had a tendency to get into trouble with the powers that be: Paconius Agrippinus was banished, Canus was executed, and Musonius Rufus was exiled, not once but twice. Seneca also got into trouble: Emperor Claudius condemned him to death for (allegedly) committing adultery. The sentence was commuted to exile to the island of Corsica. When Seneca returned from exile, Nero was emperor, and Seneca became one of his principal advisers. Nero started behaving erratically, though, and subsequently condemned Seneca to death for (allegedly) conspiring against him.

Seneca was given the choice of either killing himself or being killed by someone else. He chose the former option. Friends and family were allowed to be present during his final moments. When some of them wept, he responded by chastising them for abandoning their Stoicism, just when it would have been quite useful. He embraced his wife and cut the veins in his arms— but didn't die. Because of old age and infirmity, he was a slow bleeder. He then cut the arteries in his legs, but he still didn't die. He requested poison and drank it, but again, without the desired effect. Finally he was carried into a steam bath, where he parted from life. All this time, he remained true to his Stoic principles.

If the Stoic gods were watching, they surely shed a tear on his behalf. They were themselves Stoics, after all, and as such they would have greatly appreciated the magnificence of Seneca's exit from life.

ANOTHER DAY AT THE AIRPORT

I began this book with an airport story, and I will end it with one. In early 2017, as the result of a long and improbable series of events connected with my research on Stoicism, the culture minister of France invited me to attend the opening of an exhibition at the Louvre. Not only was this a once-in-a-lifetime opportunity, but it had an element of adventure, and so I accepted the invitation.

My wife and I flew to Atlanta, where we boarded an overnight flight for what was supposed to be a weekend in Paris. The next morning, in preparation for our arrival in France, I reached for my passport—but it wasn't where I thought I had put it. I triple-checked my pockets, my carry-on luggage, my seat, and the area around where I was sitting, but nothing turned up. A flight attendant who saw me rummaging asked whether anything was wrong. I explained the passport situation, and she said, "Don't worry. This happens all the time. It's here somewhere." She began a search but had to terminate it because our plane was in its final descent. She said that after the plane landed, we would do a thorough search.

After the other passengers deplaned, the attendant began her search in earnest. She even partially disassembled my airplane seat, but to no avail. At this point, another flight attendant came back, found out what was going on, and said, "Don't worry, I'll find it." She had me empty my pockets (again). She asked if I was wearing a security belt under my clothes. "I already checked it," I said. "Let's look again," she replied, and I awkwardly pulled it out. No passport.

By this time, four other attendants had joined our search. They were poking around and making suggestions, when the plane's pilot came back to make some suggestions of his own. I was astonished and somewhat discomfited to be the object of so much attention. It was finally decided that I should deplane without my passport and wait nearby. A ground crew, they explained, would do a very thorough cleaning of the plane, and if the passport was there, they would surely find it.

They didn't. At this point I recognized the handiwork of the Stoic gods. It was a test!

PASSPORTS DON'T JUST VANISH. My theory is that between leaving the top of the jetway in Atlanta—where I had been asked to show my passport—and arriving at my seat in the airplane, I dropped it, and whoever was behind me picked it up and pocketed it, in order to sell it. Internet research indicates that passports fetch a good price on the black market.

At this point, an airport official came to escort me to the airport police station where my passport problem would be "sorted out." He said that he had contacted the U.S. embassy, which was going to send someone to help me. When that person finally arrived at the police station, he informed me that I had picked a really bad time to lose my passport. The United States, under the direction of the recently elected president Donald Trump, had refused entry to any number of foreign citizens, creating lots of extra work for their diplomatic services. As a result, there was a very good chance that the French would use my case as part of a "payback" gesture. He explained that the police were going to question me, that I would be provided with a translator, and that I should be not just polite but very, very polite.

The policeman who subsequently questioned me would have been intimidating, even if he hadn't been wearing a gun on his hip. Through the translator, I told him my story and explained that I had been invited by the French minister of culture to attend an event at the Louvre. I even showed him the engraved invitation, which I imagined was the key that would unlock the door to Paris. He glanced at it and scoffed that it was "just a piece of paper." He then asked me to sign seven different documents, all written in French. My French is pretty basic, so I asked the translator to translate them. She responded that it was just "the usual paperwork" and that I should sign. So sign I did, on the theory that a willingness to sign documents was an internationally recognized gesture of politeness.

The policeman took the documents away to consult with a higher-up. About ten minutes later, he came back, with a scowl on his face. I expected the worst, but he announced that I had been granted permission to enter France but had to get a replacement passport as quickly as possible. My guess is that because of the Louvre invitation that "meant nothing," his boss figured that to kick me out of the country would potentially be more trouble than letting me in—and so he did.

My wife had not been allowed to come back with me during the questioning. I subsequently told her what had happened and showed her copies of the documents I had signed. Her French is much better than mine, and on scanning them, she commented that I had been wise to choose deportation by plane rather than by ship, should they have found it necessary to deport me. I was utterly unaware of having made this choice!

I had arrived in Paris on a Saturday, so I had to wait till Monday to apply for a temporary passport at the U.S. embassy. On that day, my wife and I showed up there, only to discover that it was closed for American-celebrated President's Day. *A setback within a setback*, I thought. *How ingenious!*

We returned the next morning and took our place in line—it was twice as long as usual, a consequence of the embassy having been closed the day before. (This might be described as a setback caused by a setback within a setback; the Stoic gods were clearly working overtime on this one!) In this line were people who, like me, had passport problems. At that time, I was doing research for this book. It occurred to me that this was a wonderful opportunity to see how people handled setbacks, so while my wife held our place in line, I went around asking others how they came to be here.

Everyone had a setback story to tell. Some had lost their passport or had it stolen, while others had stayed in France so long that their passport had expired. As I listened to people's stories, I tried to assess how well they were doing in the aftermath of their setback. As was to be expected, many were angry and full of blame, but others seemed to have rebounded nicely.

I got my replacement passport, and that afternoon we boarded the airplane for the trip back home. The Stoic test appeared to have concluded, so I graded my performance. Because I had spent the episode in a test-taker frame of mind, I had experienced very little frustration and no anger. My emotional state can best be described as a mixture of fascination—what *would* the Stoic gods do next?—and amusement at the test's various twists and turns. I responded to many of them with—what else?—laughter.

At that point it dawned on me that because I had made it my practice to respond to setbacks by using the Stoic test strategy, I had transformed myself from a person who regarded setbacks merely as an unfortunate aspect of life into someone who both studied and appreciated them. I had, in other words, become a setback connoisseur, and I concluded that the episode I had just experienced was the setback equivalent of the finest French champagne.

I tipped my hat to the Stoic gods for their ingenuity in devising such a test. Having the pilot come back to talk to me was a nice touch, as was having the embassy closed on the day I needed it! I also thanked the gods for the gift of testing me in this manner. Not only was it an opportunity to show my Stoic stuff, but they had also handed me, on a silver platter, a setback story to tell—and a pretty good one, too, don't you think?

ACKNOWLEDGMENTS

I would like to take this opportunity to thank Wright State University for granting me the course reduction that facilitated the writing of this book. I would also like to thank Giles Anderson for finding the book a home and Quynh Do at W. W. Norton for her helpful guidance. And not to be forgotten, I would like to thank Jamie for her patience and understanding in enduring yet another spousal literary pregnancy. And yes, now that this book is behind me, those projects around the house and the other thing *will* get done. Promise!

SUGGESTIONS FOR FURTHER READING

In these pages, I have focused my attention not on the history and principles of ancient Stoic philosophy but on a specific Stoic technique: the use of the Stoic test strategy to deal with setbacks. Those interested in learning more about Stoicism are encouraged to read my *Guide to the Good Life: The Ancient Art of Stoic Joy* (New York: Oxford University Press, 2009), in which I introduce the Stoic philosophers and explain how we can put their principles to work in our own life. Those wishing a deeper understanding of Stoic philosophy should take a look at Massimo Pigliucci's excellent *How to Be a Stoic: Using Ancient Philosophy to Live a Modern Life* (New York: Basic Books, 2017). And not to be forgotten, Seneca's essays are simultaneously accessible and full of insight.

NOTES

Introduction: A Day at the Airport

1. Seneca, "On the Happy Life," in *Seneca: Moral Essays*, vol. 2, trans. John W. Basore (Cambridge, MA: Harvard University Press, 1932), III.2.

Chapter 1: Setbacks

1. Seneca, "On Anger," in *Moral and Political Essays*, trans. John M. Cooper and J. F. Procopé (Cambridge, UK: Cambridge University Press, 1995), III.26.

Chapter 2: Anger Issues

1. Seneca, "On Anger," I.2.1.

Chapter 3: Resilience

1. "Neil Armstrong's Lunar Lander Trainer Accident," YouTube, February 28, 2010, https://www.youtube.com/watch?v=OlJGQ92IgFk.
2. James R. Hansen, *First Man: The Life of Neil A. Armstrong* (New York: Simon & Schuster, 2005), 332.

3. Bethany Hamilton, Sheryl Berk, and Rick Bundschuh, *Soulsurfer: A True Story of Faith, Family, and Fighting to Get Back on the Board* (New York: Pocket Books, 2004).

4. Marianne Thamm, *I Have Life: Alison's Journey* (New York: Penguin Putnam, 1998).

5. Alison Botha, *Alison: A Tale of Monsters, Miracles and Hope*, dir. Uga Carlini (South Africa: Journeymen Pictures 2016), 51:43.

6. Roger Ebert, "Remaking My Voice," filmed March 2011 at TED2011, https://www.ted.com/talks/roger_ebert_remaking_my_voice.

7. Lou Gehrig, "Luckiest Man," National Baseball Hall of Fame website, https://baseballhall.org/discover-more/stories/baseball-history/lou-gehrig-luckiest-man.

8. Amelia Hill, "Locked-In Syndrome: Rare Survivor Richard Marsh Recounts His Ordeal," *Guardian*, August 7, 2012, https://www.theguardian.com/world/2012/aug/07/locked-in-syndrome-richard-marsh.

9. Jean-Dominique Bauby, *The Diving Bell and the Butterfly* (New York: Alfred A. Knopf, 1997), 39.

10. Mariska J. Vansteensel et al., "Fully Implanted Brain-Computer Interface in a Locked-In Patient with ALS," *New England Journal of Medicine* 375 (2016): 2060–66.

11. Theodore Roosevelt, *The Autobiography of Theodore Roosevelt* (n.p.: Renaissance Classics, 2012), 244. Roosevelt attributes this saying to an obscure yet remarkable individual named William Widener.

12. Epictetus, "Discourses," in *Discourses, Fragments, Handbook*, trans. Robin Hard (New York: Oxford University Press, 2014), I.i.31–32. I have taken liberties with the wording of this quotation.

CHAPTER 4: CAN WE BECOME MORE RESILIENT?

1. Musonius Rufus, "Lectures," in *Musonius Rufus: Lectures and Sayings*, trans. Cynthia King (n.p.: CreateSpace, 2011), 9.10.

2. Diogenes was the founder of the Cynic school of philosophy, and he is notable for the extent to which his philosophical views affected his manner of living. He is the subject of many stories that are simultaneously funny and remarkable for the insight they give us into the human condition.

3. Musonius, "Lectures," 9.4.
4. Rachel Toor, "Hearing the Voice of a 51-Year-Old Man in the Essay of a 17-Year-Old Girl," *New York Times*, October 19, 2010, https://thechoice.blogs.nytimes.com/2010/10/19/toor/.
5. In America, there is widespread evidence of grade inflation in universities. For insight into this phenomenon, see Jane Darby Menton, "Up Close: Defining the Yale College 'A,'" *Yale News*, April 11, 2013, https://yaledailynews.com/blog/2013/04/11/up-close-defining-the-yale-college-a/.

CHAPTER 5: YOU ARE OF TWO MINDS

1. "How to Be a Hero," Radiolab podcast, January 9, 2018, https://www.wnycstudios.org/story/how-be-hero/.
2. See my *Aha! The Moments of Insight that Shape Our World* (New York: Oxford University Press, 2015).

CHAPTER 6: SINKING ANCHORS

1. Daniel Kahneman, *Thinking, Fast and Slow* (New York: Farrar, Straus & Giroux, 2011), 119.
2. Fritz Strack and Thomas Mussweiler, "Explaining the Enigmatic Anchoring Effect: Mechanisms of Selective Accessibility," *Journal of Personality and Social Psychology* 73, no. 3 (1997): 437–46.
3. In 2012 the retailer JCPenney announced its plan to abandon frequent sales in favor of everyday low pricing. At the press conference in which these plans were announced, Penney CEO Ron Johnson revealed that less than 1 percent of its revenues came from full-price transactions. This is, to be sure, only one data point but a telling one.
4. Seneca, "Consolation to Marcia," in *Seneca: Dialogues and Essays*, trans. John Davie (New York: Oxford University Press, 2007), XII.

CHAPTER 7: PLAYING THE FRAME GAME

1. Kahneman, *Thinking, Fast and Slow*, 367.
2. Epictetus, *Handbook of Epictetus*, trans. Nicholas White (Indianapolis: Hackett, 1983), 30.

3. Ibid., 5.
4. Seneca, "On Anger," III.11.
5. Marcus Aurelius, *Meditations*, trans. Maxwell Staniforth (London: Penguin, 1964), VIII.47.
6. In *On Desire: Why We Want What We Want* (New York: Oxford University Press, 2006), I argued that most people want to be rich and famous in the sense that they want to be more affluent and want to improve their standing on the social hierarchy. I also argued that people seek affluence primarily because it will improve their social standing.
7. Epictetus, *Handbook of Epictetus*, 13.
8. Seneca, "On Anger," III.33.
9. Ibid., III.11. According to other sources, it was Diogenes the Cynic who said this; see Seneca, "On Anger," IIIn7.
10. See my *A Slap in the Face—Why Insults Hurt, and Why They Shouldn't* (New York: Oxford University Press, 2013).
11. "Living with Locked-In Syndrome: Michael Cubiss," *Words of Wickert*, January 18, 2013, https://wordsofwickert.wordpress.com/2013/01/18.
12. For more on the function of "police" in ancient Athens, see "Policing in Ancient Times," *Weekend Edition*, NPR, June 11, 2005, https://www.npr.org/templates/story/story.php?storyId=4699475.
13. Jean Liedloff, *The Continuum Concept: In Search of Happiness Lost* (Cambridge, MA: Perseus Books, 1975), 10.

CHAPTER 8: YOUR *OTHER* SETBACK CHALLENGE

1. Seneca, "On Anger," II.14.
2. Martin Luther King, Jr., *The Autobiography of Martin Luther King, Jr.*, ed. Clayborne Carson (New York: Warner Books, 1998), 70.
3. Robert Kastenbaum, *Death, Society, and Human Experience*, 6th ed. (Boston: Allyn & Bacon, 1998).
4. George A. Bonanno, "Loss, Trauma, and Human Resilience," *American Psychologist* 59, no. 1 (2004): 20–28.
5. Seneca, "To Polybius on Consolation," in *Seneca: Moral Essays*, vol. 2, trans. John W. Basore (Cambridge, MA: Harvard University Press, 1932), XVIII.4–5.

Chapter 9: Using the Stoic Test Strategy

1. Seneca, "On Providence," in *Seneca: Dialogues and Essays*, trans. John Davie (New York: Oxford University Press, 2007), 4.
2. Ibid.
3. Ibid., 4–5.
4. Epictetus, "Discourses," I.1.
5. Ibid., I.24.
6. Seneca, "On Providence," 5.
7. Ibid., 5.

Chapter 10: The Five-Second Rule

1. For more information on our extended family tree, see William B. Irvine, *You: A Natural History* (New York: Oxford University Press, 2018).
2. For more on the evolution of our ability to feel good and bad, see Irvine, *On Desire*.

Chapter 11: Studying for Stoic Tests

1. Seneca, "On Providence," 3–4.
2. "Lazy Bill" is an elaboration of the being referred to as my "other self" in my *Guide to the Good Life: The Ancient Art of Stoic Joy* (New York: Oxford University Press, 2009).

Chapter 12: Embracing "Failure"

1. Howard Shultz, "Starbucks: Howard Schultz," interview by Guy Raz, NPR, September 28, 2017, https://one.npr.org/?sharedMedi aId=551874532:554086519, at 20:08.
2. Tristan Walker, "The Beauty of a Bad Idea," interview by Reid Hoffman, *Masters of Scale*, episode 3, https://mastersofscale.com/tristan-walker -beauty-of-a-bad-idea/, at 0:01.
3. Ibid., at 16:45.
4. John Danner and Mark Coopersmith, "How Not to Flunk at Failure," *Wall Street Journal*, October 25, 2015, https://www.wsj.com/articles/ how-not-to-flunk-at-failure-1445824928.

CHAPTER 13: TOUGHNESS TRAINING

1. Readers familiar with my *Guide to the Good Life* will recognize toughness training as an elaboration of the "program of voluntary discomfort" introduced there.
2. Psychologists refer to this as "exposure therapy."
3. Realize that *exploring* hunger is different from merely *experiencing* it, and that any serious exploration of hunger will require firsthand experience.
4. Seneca, *Letters from a Stoic*, trans. Robin Alexander Campbell (New York: Penguin Putnam, 1969), XVIII.
5. Musonius, "Lectures," 19.
6. Seneca, *Letters from a Stoic*, XVIII.
7. Seneca, "On Anger," II.25.

CHAPTER 14: SETUPS

1. Seneca, "On Providence," 4.
2. Michael Lewis, *The Undoing Project: A Friendship That Changed Our Minds* (New York: W. W. Norton, 2017), 354.

CHAPTER 15: DEATH

1. Lewis, *Undoing Project*, 347.
2. Seneca, "On Providence," 5.
3. Seneca, "On the Tranquility of the Mind," in *Seneca: Dialogues and Essays*, trans. John Davie (New York: Oxford University Press, 2007), 14.

INDEX

acceptance, 104
Aegean Sea, 62
Africa, 75–76
afterlife, 24–25, 149
Agrippinus, Paconius, 56, 62, 171
Aguas Calientes, Peru, 89–90
Allah, 109
amyotrophic lateral sclerosis (ALS),
    50–53
anchoring effect, 75–81
ancient Greeks, 154–55
Andes Mountains, 89
anger, 35–40
    feigned, 100
    in Kübler-Ross's five stages of grief,
        104
    responding to one's own, 38–40
    as response to setback, 16
    scope of, 35–37
    as setback, 99–102
    suppression/expression of, 37–38
Apollo 8 moon mission, 41–43
Aricia (city near ancient Rome), 56
Armstrong, Neil, 41–43
Atlanta, Georgia, 171, 174

Aurelius, Marcus, 12, 84, 134
Autobiography of Martin Luther
    King, Jr., The (King, Jr.),
    100–101

bargaining, 60, 104
Bauby, Jean-Dominique, 54–55, 90
Bean, Alan, 42–43
blame, 85, 105
Blanchard, Alana, 43–44
blindness, 79
Bonanno, George, 103
Botha, Alison, 46–48
Britain, 131

Caligula, Roman emperor, 169–70
Campbell, Joseph, 129
cancer, 29, 48, 163, 166
Canus, Julius, 169–71
Chicago Sun-Times, 48
Christianity, 13, 106, 109, 164
Clarence Odbody (character), 160
Claudius, Roman emperor, 171
color blindness, 78–79
Columbia University, 103

Index